Women at the Top

Women at the Top

ACHIEVEMENT AND FAMILY LIFE

JOAN WHEELER-BENNETT

in collaboration with
Beatrice Musgrave and
Zoë Hersov

PETER OWEN · LONDON

ISBN 0 7206 0501 6

W 6326 /5 6 78

PETER OWEN LIMITED
73 Kenway Road London SW5 0RE

First British Commonwealth edition 1977
© Joan Wheeler-Bennett 1977

Printed in Great Britain by
Bristol Typesetting Co Ltd
Barton Manor St Philips Bristol

Contents

Contents

III

A Personal Preface

Despite a few brickbats from those who persist in the conviction that hard work plus brains and talent are all that women need in order to achieve a successful career (and that they have only themselves to blame for the fact that they so seldom do), it has seemed worthwhile to try to find out from those rare beings, the women at the top, to what they attribute the successes they have had. Their experience and their advice could surely light the way for others.

Encouragement has come from a number of quarters, mostly from women who are themselves struggling to achieve in many directions: 'I want to tell you how delighted I am that you are doing this investigation,' wrote one, 'it is so necessary, our circumstances are no one else's concern . . . the usual women's organizations cater for either the full-time professionals, most of whom have no children I suppose, or for the full-timers who hand their children to nannies and boarding schools.'

'Thank goodness for your concern for the rest of us,' wrote an anaesthetist, while a portrait painter said: 'This is your rather special thing – seeing how to materialize the potential in others.' Accolades such as these heartened us to persist in an investigation which cannot make claims of scientific validity or do more than push open a few doors. Some, indeed, will take the view that the millions of married women who are not in the labour statistics should be left in peace; but it is common sense that some at least of these non-taxpayers, one of the notorious untapped reservoirs in the economy, should be cajoled and winkled out of their domestic shells.

Opposition is not lacking either: 'Surely women don't need special help nowadays,' runs a typical objection. 'It is the second rate who agitate about sex discrimination. Will women never be satisfied? Must they always blame their failures on the short-comings of others?'

7

'Many women are frustrated in their careers because they just aren't good enough.' Some successful career women are among those who adopt this kind of line. There may, of course, be truth in such accusations in some instances, but they do not provide even a partial answer to the question : 'What happened to half the school-leaving population, the half that did so well in the examinations, the female half?'

No one denies that hard work plus brains and talent are the normal ingredients of success. But if it can be agreed also that females are endowed at birth with much the same potential, in respect to these qualities, as males, then it must be a matter of wonder and concern that they are so often absent from places of power and influence later in life. This book is intended to alert the reader to the difficulties that beset any woman who seeks achievement in what is still a man's world, while fulfilling the natural, desirable role as homemaker. Even so, many women are managing to combine the two functions happily and successfully, and in describing how they set about it we hope that more may be stimulated to do likewise. But we accept that many more will continue to feel that the effort is too great and will forgo the struggle to achieve public recognition as well as private satisfaction.

J.E.W-B.

Introduction

The background

In the early 1960s, when many married women with professional qualifications were denied the opportunity to work outside the home because they felt unable to combine family obligations with what was then nearly always full-time employment, a group of working wives banded together to influence public opinion in favour of part-time work. The group aimed to encourage women, and employers, to find new career patterns for married women : a flexible, shorter working day to allow for the demands of family life, and opportunities for promotion despite maternity absence. The group was motivated then, as now, by the observation that the talents and training of many women were being wasted. And the single most important explanation for this wastage, it was realized, was the choice that faced women : between all or nothing, between full-time work or no work at all. Calling itself initially the Women's Information and Study Centre, the group undertook to publish information designed to encourage women to train for, and seek, employment that could be combined with looking after a family; to persuade employers and professional institutions that part-time work was not only the sensible, but often the *only* way for a woman to combine a family with a career; and to convince them that – if the woman had skills to offer that were needed and in short supply – this could ultimately be to everyone's benefit.

*Comeback,** a 40-page directory to a wide variety of professions, was published in 1964. This was followed in 1969 by *Working Wonders*† and in 1972 by another full-length book,

---

* *Comeback: A Guide for the Educated Woman Returning to Work,* Women's Information and Study Centre, 1964.
† Pat Williams in collaboration with Joan Wheeler-Bennett, Zoë Hersov, Beatrice Musgrave and Tessa Smith, *Working Wonders: The Success Story of Wives Engaged in Professional Work Part-Time,* Hodder & Stoughton, 1969.

9

Women at Work,‡ both dealing with the problems of married women in professional work and offering some solutions. In the years following publication of *Comeback*, the group also sponsored conferences in conjunction with the National Advisory Centre on Careers for Women, prepared and analysed 250 questionnaires about part-time work (used in *Working Wonders*), kept in close touch with developments in the fields of training and employment, and contributed to the debate about the working wife's role – both privately and in the media.

Since the group's inception in 1963, many changes have taken place in social attitudes and employment patterns. There is now greatly increased awareness of the need for women to contribute their education and skills to society. There is also less prejudice, new opportunities have been created in training and employment, hours are more flexible and a fresh generation of family women is now accepting, almost as a commonplace, the right to decide whether and how to work. Yet, in spite of a vastly different climate of opinion, there are still only a few women right at the top, numerically insignificant in relation to the attention they tend to attract to themselves. Why should this be so? The present investigation was undertaken in order to discover some of the answers.

Why investigate top women now?

It has been agreed for some time that more women should be encouraged to achieve positions where their voices can be heard and their influence felt. Yet employment statistics show that the proportion of women in skilled and executive occupations is actually decreasing, despite the increase in educational qualifications and the generally more favourable conditions regarding recruitment and promotion. The setting up of the Equal Opportunities Commission in 1975 has given new urgency to the question. It will undoubtedly hasten the search for 'token' women to be appointed to positions of authority from which they have so

‡ Beatrice Musgrave and Joan Wheeler-Bennett (eds.), *Women at Work: Combining Family with a Career*, including *Comeback: A Directory to the Professions*, Peter Owen, 1972.

far been absent (advisory boards and committees) and to participate in training schemes and management. But such appointments are more likely to meet the letter of the law than its spirit;
it is all too likely that, to begin with, women will have to be
conjured up whose qualifications are visible status rather than
proven merit, whose appointments are politic rather than professional. The women in line for promotion are often the ones
least willing to put themselves forward, or least prepared to
benefit from legal equality at higher levels. Even though it may
be agreed that – in spite of high unemployment – the need for
top-quality professional and managerial skills has never been
greater, and that women can supply some of these skills, will the
right women come forward to present themselves? If, as is often
assumed, it is outside circumstances that have so far militated
against the appointment and promotion of women to top jobs,
will the new legislation automatically redress the imbalance by
removing the obstacles? Are drive and ambition held back only
by opportunity and are suitably qualified women now going to
present themselves in numbers for posts demanding a high degree
of commitment and responsibility? The experience of the women
in this survey offers no such assurances. And while these questions
have still to be answered, listening to women who are already
successfully working at a high level will help to shed light on the
whole controversial topic of 'equal opportunities' and what these
are likely to mean in practice.

About this survey

Nearly ten years after we first received the completed questionnaires on which the findings of *Working Wonders* are based, we
sent out a follow-up questionnaire to sixty-five selected women,
all of them highly qualified. We asked them whether they felt that
they had realized their original ambition and, if so, what had
helped them to do so; also, what – if any – had been the price
they had had to pay. If their careers had fallen short of expectation, we asked them to enumerate the reasons. We suggested
that these might include children and other family commitments,
personal reservations, bad luck or bad health, lack of husband's

support, lack of financial incentive, or prejudice against women in the profession or elsewhere. Of the sixty-five selected, most had been in their thirties ten years ago, had small children and were working part-time. Now, with children mostly in their teens or older, more than half are working full-time, although most describe their working hours as having a good deal of flexibility. As in the original *Comeback*, the range of occupations is broadly based; it cannot, however, claim to be fully representative, given the fact that women are much more to the fore in certain professions than in others. The experiences and opinions of these women are summed up in a general text covering different topics and interspersed with the comments of individual participants. The second part of the book reproduces complete interviews with a number of outstandingly successful women whose ideas in the main bear out the conclusions reached in the first part, but who also offer some interesting and highly individual opinions. The final section draws attention to the need for change, based on the evidence of the survey, and offers some proposals for action.

Our assumption has been that change usually comes from the top; that it is useful to give examples that encourage and models that can be followed; that the few who have conspicuously succeeded can provide pointers for those who have not or who may be reluctant to try.

The present survey is confined to women who are, or have been, married and who have children – the circumstances in which women now most commonly find themselves. Virtually all women, married or single, with children or without, assume family responsibilities of some kind, either from choice or because society expects it of them. But the situation of those who bear and rear children is radically different from those who do not, and the concept of the family as the core of society is still the most stabilizing influence within western society. The family orientation of these women is therefore the norm.

The women who have been interviewed represent a particular generation which can speak only for itself. It seems likely that patterns of work sharing, both inside and outside the home, will be somewhat different in the years to come. But radical alteration in the focus of responsibility upon women in the home seems unlikely. There is not the slightest evidence that society will expect men to take primary responsibility for the care of family dependants or that women generally are ready to divest themselves of their traditional role.

I

The Pursuit of Success

Historically, women with ambition have tended to enter the professions rather than industry and commerce. And in the professions it has been the creative ones (writing, broadcasting, advertising, journalism, architecture, design) and the traditional 'caring' ones (medicine, teaching, social work) rather than the so-called 'numerate' ones (accountancy, surveying, land-management, stockbroking, banking) which have attracted women. This explains the preponderance of certain professions in our survey, which follows up the careers of a number of women who were working successfully in 1969. While it is recognized that the position is slowly changing, helped by increased awareness and tolerance on the part of society, and by changes inside the professions as well as through the legislative reforms of the Equal Opportunities Commission, there are good reasons to believe that the high representation of women in certain professions is likely to continue. Some evidence for this belief appears in the pages that follow.

In trying to find causes for the conspicuous absence of women from top jobs, various reasons are usually cited, including inequality of opportunity, social prejudice, and lack of such personal qualities as drive and entrepreneurial talent. The Political and Economic Planning Survey *Women in Top Jobs*, published in 1971, pointed out that women generally are not seekers of power or status, being willing to carry responsibility without salary or title, and that they are less competitive and less persistent than men. Our aim when conducting a survey of sixty-five women working successfully at the higher levels of a number of different professions, was to establish what, in their opinion, constituted curbs to top level success and to discover the qualities and circumstances that enabled certain women to surmount these.

CURBS TO SUCCESS

It would appear that the main obstacle to the realization of high professional goals, as well as the principal curb to ambition, is the role – with all its consequences – in which the majority of women see themselves and are seen, and which is felt to be natural and right. This is as wives and mothers who assume prime responsibility for their homes and children and who, if a choice has to be made, put the needs of their families, including husbands, before their own. For all but the most exceptionally determined or lucky women, this must mean less than total dedication to their careers, at least during the early stages of childbearing and rearing. The need to interrupt a career for a while, to work less than full-time, or to work a flexible timetable, is not yet compatible with promotion within the usual career structures; too often it militates against appointing women to the senior posts which they merit. This kind of prejudice can be overcome only when a woman's career span is seen as a whole and employers begin to make the adjustments, at certain stages, that will enable women to make the fullest contribution possible during their overall working lives.

Ambition tempered by woman's role

It is interesting that, as a result of having to modify their goals in order to do justice to their family responsibilities, many women deny their ambition, as if ambition and singlemindedness were qualities not compatible with being a woman. For the same reason they often seem to play down their success and achievement, in the face of evidence to the contrary:

'I really don't like the word success; prefer satisfaction.' – *Social Worker*

'My ambition has been in a different key: to find a job which stretched my mind and which I found satisfying.' – *Economic Planner*

'I have been promoted beyond my expectations.' – *Principal Lecturer*

'Certainly I'm not at the top, but in any case I'm not cut out for that. I have achieved exactly what I wanted and two sons as well.' – *Anthropologist*

In a few women with strong ambitions the role in which they find themselves may be almost resented:

'I have had to limit my practice and ambitions and put husband and family first.' – *Barrister*

Others accept the need for compromise and occasionally stress the benefits in terms of a more balanced personality or a richer, more fulfilled life:

'I am on the penultimate rung of the ladder and quite content to accept the limitation of a family.' – *Medical Consultant*

'I am not at the top but never had any ambition to be. Accommodating husband and children is essential.' – *Clinical Psychologist*

'I am less ambitious professionally as I get other satisfaction from my family. I don't need to reach the top of my profession.'
– *Medical Clinician*

'My aim is a fulfilled life, not to get to the top of my career.'
– *Senior Civil Servant*

'The neurotic component of my ambition has become modified and I am quite content to accept the limitation of a career and family.' – *Consultant Psychiatrist*

'I wanted a family and children so writing had to suffer. I will be all the better for having had a family.' – *Author*

Priority given to children

In their work, many women are prepared to make adjustments to their timetables at the cost of promotion or greater responsibility, if they have the choice. This is to ensure that their children's needs are fully met :

I am used as a reliable emergency helper but carry no real responsibility. I limit my work so that I can be home for the children. Preparing children for future lives is more important for a woman than mere success hunting for herself.' – *Freelance Book Editor*

'I do not always follow through professional invitations involving residence or trips abroad because it means too much time away from the children. I decline most evening commitments. I do not find time to publish much. I am confined to posts within reach of my house. What is more important is that my family is truly happy and my children receive adequate attention and love.' – *Psychotherapist*

'Frustrations have arisen at work through opportunities missed because children have to be collected from school. But a stable, reliable home front is essential.' – *Gallery Director*

Not all jobs, however, permit a degree of flexibility where adjustment is possible. Often a more exclusive commitment to work is demanded and the care of children has to be largely delegated. While this delegation may be a free choice in some cases, suited to the particular temperament of the mother, in many others it is forced on a woman because career ladders require close attention at every rung and to let go, even temporarily, puts a woman at a disadvantage. Many women who have chosen in favour of their children, accept the consequent career setback as inevitable; to others it is a cause for disappointment and regret :

'I gave up work for family commitments, a step most reluctantly taken but undoubtedly the right one. I intend to start doing something again in a few years, preferably at home.' – *Ex-Managing Director*

'I gave up medical social work six weeks before the expected birth of my first son. I felt at the time that I would like to return after he was born, but as soon as I had him I faltered – I daren't. Like many other earnest young mothers of the period I had read (and badly misconstrued) the work of John Bowlby. So I stayed at home to ensure the emotional well-being of my child, at great cost, at times, to my own! – *Sociologist*

Not only do the majority of women feel that the demands of a career should not take precedence over their children – and make some compromise as a result – but also they want to retain the responsibility for bringing them up. Maternal feelings run as deep in intellectual women as in others and bring with them rewards that few women seem willing to forgo. Nor does this change suddenly when children are out of the nursery stage. Feelings of guilt and regret at not having spent enough time with the children generally or when they were young, are commonly voiced, and not only by those who work :

'If I had my time over again I would have spent more time with the children and felt less worried about being out of the profession for a bit.' – *Consultant Child Psychiatrist*

'When I was working more or less full-time I was racked with guilt at not having spent more time with the children.' – *Gallery Director*

'Sacrifices include not being able to spend time with my children when school play or sports day clash with business appointment; also during school holidays.' – *Public Relations Director*

Looking after children must therefore be seen as a fundamental and continuing concern which cannot be completely delegated. It is a longer process than is generally admitted – a fact that has probably received too little attention. Women themselves have been influenced by the facile assumption that prime responsibility ends when a child goes to school.

Care of dependants and invalids

Children are only part of the story, albeit a dominant one during the early years. It is usually true that, as children become less dependent they leave a mother freer to develop her own career. But for some women it is not so simple : as children grow up grandparents and other elderly relatives grow old, and one kind of dependency often succeeds another.

The care of elderly relatives, and of invalids in general, customarily falls to women, by necessity if not by choice. Not one of the women in this survey who referred to elderly dependants questioned the assumption that the duty of caring for them should fall to her :

'In recent years I have gradually increased my work commitments and as my sons grew up I felt free to pursue work interests fully. I am now a little alarmed to find that an aged mother is the next item on my life-and-work see-sawing agenda. The cost to my peace of mind battling against pressures to demote me to a home help (invaluable ladies as they are, I do not consider my own skills would be fulfilled in being one) could be high if things go badly.' – *Sociologist*

'I thought I was getting organized to find more time for writing (I have been commissioned to write a textbook) but the increasing frailty of my elderly parents has involved my sister and myself in a good deal of extra time in order to maintain them in the dignity and comfort of their home. However much help one obtains or arranges, domestic or nursing, one's frequent presence is essential.' – *Psychotherapist*

'I have had no ambition to take on further responsibility at work as I am caring for my elderly mother, which I want to do.' – *Social Worker*

These women reinforce the current vogue for 'community care' which, when translated, means keeping people in their own homes and out of institutions. The theory behind this is clearly humane and sensible because it sustains the person as an individual and reduces institutionalization. But for every individual who will come to enjoy 'community care', one may be sure that there will be at least one woman at home doing the caring. And unless the community, in its caring, provides supportive services to go into the home, the greater part of day-to-day care and responsibility for those who cannot look after themselves will be carried by the mothers, wives and daughters in the family. This has always been the case and seems likely to continue so.

A number of women would like to see some change in the next generation, but in this connection the education of boys, and the husband's co-operation in psychological rather than practical terms, were the only suggestions made.

As in the case of children, women again show themselves willing to take full responsibility. Too little thought has as yet been given to the multiplicity and open-endedness of a woman's family role, probably because this is socially convenient and spares others the burden of guilt.

Husbands and domesticity

Most of the women questioned belong to an economic group in which husbands usually provide enough security to cushion their wives against the immediate need to work. Often, their jobs also confer the status which a wife might otherwise seek outside. This role of the husband as principal provider leads to the general acceptance of the necessity to give a husband's career – and his other needs – priority. One wife sums this up :

'I am lucky because I don't have to earn more from economic necessity. My husband works long hours and I don't think husbands and wives can both do this without undue stress and damage to health.' – *Architect*

Another comments :

'One of us has to make the final decision; if we cannot agree it is better for the man to decide.' – *Journalist*

Perhaps the most important aspect of giving precedence to the husband is the location of the family home. Many of the participants have had to make a choice taking this into account at some point in their careers :

'I have had to move overseas with my husband at a critical time of my career.' – *Economist*

'A woman is expected to move locality with her husband's changes of job. In my case this meant that I had to change speciality.' – *Psychiatrist*

'I started on an academic career at Cambridge which I had to abandon, going into the Civil Service at which I was successful.

Since I married I have had to make what I could of a career which could be done anywhere as my husband moves about.' – *Novelist*

One may assume that this particular problem lessens in later years when children grow up and the husband has passed the peak of his career. But by then a woman's chances of reaching hers may also have receded. On the other hand some women do flourish later in life, when their career becomes the more prominent.

While the help and co-operation of husbands was widely praised, several women voiced the need for a change in attitudes, including the education of men :

'Social attitudes change slowly and many men do not accept that women need to work and will not hear of women working full-time.' – *Barrister*

'There are social pressures for a wife to cushion her husband but not vice versa.' – *Psychiatrist*

'One of the difficulties is the attitude of society which still too readily assumes that a woman's place is exclusively in the home.' – *Architect and Senior Tutor*

The reason for a husband's lack of support may well be his fear that the home will suffer. It is still generally assumed that the principal responsibility for running the home should rest with the wife, a fact most wives accept but nevertheless find a great obstacle to the pursuit of their careers :

'Running husband, family and job is utterly and exhaustingly demanding.' – *Architect*

'My chances are less than those of male colleagues not because of prejudice but because of conflicting demands on my time and energy. Running a household leaves me little time for my own research and absolutely no chance of concentrating my attention on it for a reasonably extended period.' – *University Lecturer*

Domestic help of the calibre needed to replace a wife in the home is not only difficult to find but a heavy, often disproportionate burden on the family budget. Some women insisted on the need to pay a great deal of money for adequate help to look after children, others questioned whether it was financially worthwhile. There was widespread agreement about the need for tax reform and the 'recognition of such extra vital expenses as domestic help'.

None of the women specifically asked that their husbands should do more in the home, although many advocated more and better services outside – in the form of crèches, day nurseries, school transport, play facilities, holiday camps, and domestic and child-care co-operatives. The suggestion that homemakers and mothers should be paid for their work was also mentioned.

The most hopeful sign of change for the better is the increased acceptance of husbands and wives sharing home tasks. This is certainly gaining ground among a younger generation of married couples and may well turn out to be one of the more significant aspects of change in the future.

Lack of flexibility

The lack of opportunity to work part-time or to a flexible timetable, at least during some stages of their careers, inhibits many women from setting their sights high. School holidays, half-terms, sports days and illnesses must all be coped with. Time to be around to talk is important but difficult to quantify. The varying aspects of mothering as well as of parental care in general all point to the need for women's career structures to be flexible. Lack of flexibility goes a long way towards explaining the relative absence of women from management and positions of leadership in commerce and industry – with their more rigid career structures and timetables – and the persistent drift towards the professions. Many women, determined to do justice to the needs of their families, can only work when hours are flexible. They put less emphasis on the total number of hours they work than on the fact that these can be adjusted to fit in with home commitments. This accounts for the preponderance in this survey – and in general – of women who work on a sessional basis or are self-employed, such as editors, copywriters and journalists, tutors and university lecturers, architects, and members of the medical and para-medical profession. For some women this basis offers the ideal solution :

'I could at any time have returned to working in a publishing firm but have preferred to stay at home because of the pleasure of working this way.' – *Freelance Editor*

Others are fortunate enough to be in senior positions in certain professions where flexibility seems to be relatively the order of the day. Senior Civil Servants and academics are among these :

'I am remarkably free to plan my hours. I have a fellowship and college lectureship, exactly what I wanted.' – *University Lecturer*

It is in the middle ranks, where the individual has little control over working arrangements, and before enough experience and expertise have been acquired, that the incompatibility of home demands and a career most often arises. Untold numbers of women must in consequence be prevented from ever reaching the point in a career that brings increased freedom.

Employers and the public still tend to consider flexible hours or part-time work as second best, when it could so easily work to their advantage :

'The advantages to an employer of employing part-time women who work in their own time need stressing and publicizing. In fact we are good value for money.' – *Architect*

'The important thing about working women is that employers must learn to be more flexible about part-time arrangements. This will only happen as they learn the value of their female employees.' – *Psychiatrist*

The truth of this is attested by a number of women who are able to offer special skills or who work in shortage professions :

'My promotion as a part-timer may be a precedent. Success is due to having a skill in demand.' – *Civil Servant (Assistant Secretary)*

'I acquired a Ph.D. and am a recognized expert in my own field. Part-time work has been easy to come by as clinical psychology is so desperately needed.' – *Clinical Psychologist*

'I have an interesting and well-paid job with some flexibility of hours. I am in a field where I can work part-time and yet take clinical responsibility and long-term care of my patients.' – *Clinical Researcher*

'Part-time social work gained ground because of the sheer need for employees.' – *Social Work Administrator*

We have long argued, with plenty of evidence in support (see *Working Wonders*), that less than full-time work is what the great majority of professional women with families want. In fact less than half the women in this survey are working part-time, but the other half work what is variably described as a 'flexible' or 'nearly full-time' schedule. It is interesting to speculate on the reasons why women who said ten years ago that they wanted to continue working part-time indefinitely have now taken to working full-time in one form or another. Are they women with greater-than-average drive who have been willing – and able – to overcome obstacles and pay the price? Or have they been the lucky ones?

An interrupted career or a late start

Interrupting one's career often means difficulty in re-entering or inability to pick up where one left off, and the consequent abandonment of early ambitions.

'Despite the fact that I am now better qualified than when I was first employed, I shall find it more difficult to be employed than if I were beginning my career.' – *University Lecturer*

It is not surprising to be told, therefore :

'If you want to go to the top, don't drop out when you have children.' – *Historical Researcher*

It is unlikely that the need to take time off for childbearing is an insurmountable obstacle to singleminded and dedicated women. Such women accept the consequent need to hand over much of the care of their homes and children to others in order to apply themselves to the demands of a career. But the great majority of women lack this singleminded resolve, largely because of their need for involvement with their children and families in the early years, but also because they may not yet have found where their true interests lie :

'I did not have any clear aims, partly because of family commitments. I feel I will be more ambitious and adventurous in a few years.' – *Copywriter*

'I did not find the area of work which really attracted me (urban planning) until I was in my late thirties. By then it was not possible to move seriously in that direction. It is important to know your mind early on and to be singleminded.' – *Economist*

'Marriage stopped me pursuing my original ambition but how keen was I? I feel I have developed much more in my forties partly because I've put myself to the test. A late start is necessary for some of us.' – *Social Work Administrator*

The Equal Opportunities Commission will undoubtedly seek ways to circumvent the problem of the interrupted career by means such as long-term leave of absence. But in this connection it is worth reflecting on the effects of legislation that has been introduced in Sweden and East Germany to encourage women to assume more leadership in government and industry. It is early to draw conclusions but observers have already noted that women are assuming the same domestic responsibilities as before although they are taking on more outside work. It is thus not surprising that they are not conspicuous as parliamentarians or captains of industry, even in these countries. The introduction of maternity and child-care leave in Sweden, to be interchangeable between fathers and mothers, may break through the male resistance to domestic responsibility, but few women there give signs of wanting to give up their domestic roles altogether. Even with new legislation, therefore, it seems unlikely that there will be dramatic changes in the foreseeable future.

Prejudice

In the creative or 'caring' professions, in which most of the women in this group find themselves, prejudice is not likely to present an overt obstacle to promotion, as is the case in certain other professions. For example, it does not operate by actually debarring women from on-the-job training and experience, as is the case in certain industries, or by providing so little encouragement that only the exceptionally interested or determined persist (as in surveying, land-management, actuarial work or stockbroking). Here it is more likely to manifest itself at the higher levels, when a woman of ability has nearly reached the top.

Non-eligibility for promotion as a matter of declared policy, as related by one woman, is probably no longer possible because of legislation on equal opportunities :

'I was told : "This (merchandising) company does not approve of women in senior management or at director level." ' – *Public Relations Director*

However, it persists in more subtle ways :

'There is unadmitted prejudice against a woman to reach further than shoulder height.' – *Associate Director, Advertising Agency*

Promotion of women to the top still seems to be affected by the lack of objective tests for competence and the expectation that they must prove themselves at every stage :

'I have had to demonstrate very clearly at all levels that I am fully qualified as well as capable of filling my job. For example, I have had to take a quite unnecessary doctorate in order to obtain fair promotion.' – *Scientific Officer*

It also seems inevitable that concentration of men in top jobs must result in a bias in their favour :

'You have to be very committed and typically better than any man to get the same job.' – *Pro-Vice-Chancellor*

'It took others considerably longer to accept me than if I had been a man. Only exceptional women get to the top, whereas very ordinary men do.' – *Managing Director, Publishing Firm*

'A woman has to be much better qualified than a man.' – *Psychotherapist*

The fear that a woman will do her job less well because she cannot work to a rigid nine-to-five schedule or because of her domestic responsibilities, still colours the views of many employers :

'The first question at an interview is nearly always : "Do you have domestic help?", so I know I am up against prejudice. This makes me anxious and the interview is not what it should be.' – *Psychotherapist*

Women are far less likely to come up against prejudice where career patterns are most visible and women are not excluded from senior appointments, as in the Civil Service :

'I am privileged because, in common with many, I have experienced no discrimination.' – *Senior Inspector, Civil Service*

or in small firms, where promotion is less keenly contested :

'Opportunities are better in small firms.' – *Economist*

In the end, prejudice in its specific forms is only evidence of wider social attitudes and the low expectation of women's career potential. As one contributor says :

'If I hadn't been conditioned by society's expectation of women, might I not have set my sights higher or differently?' – *Consultant Child Psychiatrist*

THE ANATOMY OF SUCCESS

When all the circumstantial problems are taken into account, the surprise is that so many women do achieve success. But to distil a neat prescription from the experience of these women is impossible. At best one can attempt to single out some of the ingredients which, separately or combined, are regarded as important by those who consider themselves successful.

Among natural endowments, good health – and energy – are rated highly :

'Good health is the most important quality.' – *Economist*

'A prime essential is good health.' – *Lecturer*

'One does need energy.' – *Senior Lecturer*

Brains and talent may be obvious and implicit requisites in any profession; talent is clearly at a premium in a creative one :

'I have talent, never give up.' – *Novelist*

'You can't measure success in writing as you can the chairmanship of ICI for instance. Those women not realizing their ambition may simply not have had the talent.' – *Writer*

Taste and judgement are also valued :

'I had to learn a lot before I could exercise my taste and judgement.' – *Managing Director*

'My job is very responsible and interesting, requiring judgement.'
– *Housing Manager*

Persistence, singlemindedness, determination and discipline all receive attention :

'It is necessary to persist and not to be put off by difficulties.' – *Medical Scientific Officer*

'Individuals who are able and determined will always succeed.' – *Senior Lecturer*

'I would single out discipline and singlemindedness.' – *Painter*

'Achievement really means hard work and strong motivation.' – *Social Worker*

'Hard work and self-discipline.' – *Public Relations Director*

The insistence on hard work is almost universal :

'There is no real substitute for hard work.' – *Economist*

'I worked terribly hard but always do. I had the confidence (or cheek) to apply for a top job.' – *Headmistress*

'I achieved as high as I aimed, in fact higher. I attribute my success to hard work.' – *Architect*

'Hard work. I was prepared to try six different specialities, moving locality with my husband's changes of job.' – *Consultant Psychiatrist*

Several women couple hard work with the need to organize oneself and to sort out priorities :

'A lot of effort and organization on a personal level are necessary.'
– *Senior Lecturer*

B

'I have achieved my ambition to become a child psychiatrist and chairman of a department for children and parents at my clinic. It is a question of sorting your priorities and being prepared to pay the price.' – *Consultant Psychiatrist*

Dedication is also implied :

'It's a question of choosing a job you really like and you willingly give your whole time to it because you enjoy it.' – *Managing Editor*

Only one woman, however, recommended putting the job before the family :

'It is necessary to get involved in the job and be prepared to put job before family.' – *Economist*

The need to be better at the job than a man, already noted in the section on prejudice, acts as a further spur to hard work :

'Basically you must do each stage of your job well and often better than the men.' – *Television Producer*

The recommendation to work hard is not linked with the need to work full-time by any of these women, many of whom work flexible hours. This again emphasizes the point that long hours do not necessarily mean rigid hours.

'I work at home half the week so my hours are flexible and I can take the occasional day off. But I have always worked very hard, often in the evenings and through weekends.' – *Editorial Director*

Career patterns vary widely but knowing what they wanted to do early has given some women a start over others :

'If you know what you want you are half-way there.' – *Architect*

'My recommendation: know your mind early.' – *Urban Planner*

They gained work experience as well as 'paper' qualifications, which meant postponement of children, but established them in their careers:

'I waited ten years before having children to enable me to continue with the same job.' – *Public Relations Director*

'It is important to be in an established enough position so that freewheeling for a few years won't matter.' – *Architect*

'I got specialist qualifications in medicine before having three children.' – *Consultant Psychiatrist*

'I was thirty-four and earning well by the time we had children.' – *University Lecturer*

'If you plan to interrupt your career you must get the necessary qualifications and basic experience before you do so.' – *Senior Inspector, Civil Service*

'Try and qualify as something. Try not to get married too young or before you have received training and worked in at least one job. It is harder to do the work if you have to get your training and working experience after you are married and have a family.' – *Architect and Senior Tutor*

'Obviously one can build on the foundation of a good education and training, but my advice to any ambitious woman would be to finish her initial training before marriage and to gain some professional experience before leaving work to start a family.' – *Principal Lecturer, College of Education*

'I believe that the qualification of women before childbearing is a must – perhaps the most important investment in their own future that they can make. I am not sure most young women see the importance of this even now.' – *Sociologist*

In this connection, the importance of establishing a reputation and making useful contacts should not be overlooked:

'Any medical practitioner should find the field that interests her and get experience and contacts (which are more important than qualifications) before having children.' – *Clinical Researcher*

It is known that women are likely to lose confidence and to feel that their skills are getting rusty during an extended break, adding a psychological to a real disadvantage. The need to 'keep going' in some form or other was endorsed by many:

'Even when home commitments are very demanding, one must keep in touch, by either part-time or freelance work.' – *Architect*

'However high or otherwise one aspires, I am sure it is vital to keep in touch in some way, such as voluntary work. I did a variety of things after I married.' – *Social Work Administrator*

'I left my publishing job after seven years just before my daughter was born and returned to work (part-time) for a different publisher, six years later, when my son started nursery school. In the interval I kept going with freelance editing, translating and evening-class teaching.' – *Editorial Director*

However, keeping in touch does not insure against the loss of valuable experience or opportunities for promotion. Realizing this, most of the women who consider that they have achieved success, contrived to keep going with hardly a break – despite the admitted strain:

'My own experience has led me to believe that continuing in some form of work full-time gives one the experience necessary to compete with others.' – *Senior Principal, Civil Service*

'I am one rank below board level. I think it is very necessary to keep going throughout, not to stop – except very briefly – when having children.' – *Associate Director, Advertising Agency*

Natural endowments, motivation and other qualities of character in combination with hard work go a long way, but they leave out two additional ingredients, one of them important, the other vital.

The first is luck, or chance – in the form of an unexpected opportunity, a profession in demand or an accommodating employer :

'I have been particularly lucky in being on the spot.' – *Lecturer*

' "Success" has come more by luck than judgement.' – *Television Interviewer*

'I was lucky (or wise) to specialize in an expanding subject.' – *Psychiatrist*

'I am not special, just lucky.' – *Medical Clinician*

'I was lucky in that my employer was looking for somebody to work for him in a very small way (two to three hours a week) at just about the time when I was ready to return. The job and the firm really expanded together.' – *Editorial Director*

The need to seize opportunities is also mentioned :

'I have always grasped any chance to take on more responsibility.' – *Principal Lecturer*

'An aptitude for building on to chance openings is essential.' – *Employment Agency Director*

That so much should be left to chance is alarming but true. There is still a wide gap between expectations engendered by a woman's early education and the experience of her working life.

The vital ingredient is a supportive husband. Without this, it would have been almost impossible for these women, with their desire to put family first, to achieve the balance and stability needed to function effectively in a job :

'My husband has to be committed to my working.' – *Pro-Vice-Chancellor*

'Marry the right man – and marry him late.' – *Lecturer*

'I have the support of my husband.' – *Television Interviewer*

'I have been fortunate in having a loving husband.' – *Housing Manager*

'Having a husband determined to make it possible for me to have a professional career has been essential to my success. Women of my generation lack confidence.' – *University Professor*

'You need your husband's complete support if you are going to have your own career.' – *Psychiatrist*

On a more down-to-earth note, a husband who can support a woman in a more practical sense is also considered to have made an important contribution:

'Marry wisely; that is, a husband who can support you.' – *Novelist*

'Women whose husbands can support them through the "domestic" years are privileged in that they can try out different options.' – *Social Worker*

The price they pay

It would not be appropriate to make much of the problems and sacrifices that often accompany success, as these women make so little of them themselves. But the cost must be considered. Apart from feelings of regret and guilt at not having spent more time with children – already mentioned earlier – there may be other drawbacks that affect family life:

'A high price has been paid in many ways: rush in family life, children lacking confidence and problems about money that don't arise when a wife is at home.' – *University Professor*

Similarly, social life may suffer in some way:

'Adult activities must be curtailed, like going out and entertaining.' – *Civil Servant*

'I have had to neglect friendships which I might regret one day.'
– *Painter*

'It helps if you give up wanting to be liked by everyone.' –
Barrister

'I could not put up with drawbacks of lack of time for hobbies
and social life unless I were doing a job that is socially useful and
morally sound.' – *Lecturer*

'Anything you devote yourself to means that your life is narrowed
down a bit and my social life and outside interests have suffered
considerably.' – *Editor*

'Often work intrudes in the evening and at weekends.' –
Company Chairman

Fatigue and general health problems are mentioned occasionally, but in a minor key:

'The cost is physical tiredness.' – *Lecturer*

'Overwork has resulted in certain health problems, for example
high blood pressure; several miscarriages might have been a
result.' – *Public Relations Director*

Most women seem to accept the cost willingly:

'One pays the price in terms of having to accept less than ideal
standards in the home in terms of order; also one accepts fatigue
as inevitable. I don't accept this as a high price but it exists.' –
Principal Medical Officer

'I have virtually no social life but do not regret this.' – *Research Fellow*

Only one woman admitted that it prevented her from aiming higher :

'I would have been more successful if willing to pay high price.' – *Examiner and Novelist*

When considering the negative aspects of dedication to a career, one must remember the women who are not in this survey because they lack the qualification of keeping a husband as well as a career and children. Cause and effect are almost impossible to determine, but the University Reader who replied that she was disqualified from being included undoubtedly speaks for a proportion of women for whom the price has been too high :

'I have paid the price of a broken marriage with subsequent problems and now general isolation from social life. As my children have also suffered, this hurts me too.'

But against this casualty must be set the majority who claim that their marriages – and their lives generally – have been happier as a result of their career interests, and would not have had it any other way.

IN CONCLUSION

The commonest denominator is balance – the ability to weigh up many ingredients, to keep the equilibrium between the demands made upon these successful women and their capacity to meet them. The balance is not always easily maintained; an element of guilt is often acknowledged to be the by-product of doing many things at once, and an awareness of community as well as family obligations makes some who cannot meet them feel neglectful.

It is accepted that a price has to be paid : most often exhaustion, occasionally the cutting of standards in the house, often the curtailment of social life. But it would not occur to these family women to make drastic changes. Despite the drawbacks, they count themselves fortunate in having resolved the competing demands of work and family life. The solutions for combining two lives in one are individual in detail, but in general they have more to do with hard work, ingenuity and luck than with 'super-humanity'.

All the participants show a degree of flexibility in their working timetable. Those who work fewer than the usual number of hours (about half) have often had to forfeit normal status and promotion.

In their search for achievement in the widest sense, the majority find that the topmost rewards elude them. Not all willingly accept as inevitable the limitation in career prospects imposed on them as a result of their roles as mothers and family women.

Too many of the brightest and best still cluster on the foothills without ever reaching the top.

II

Fifteen Individual Portraits

The fifteen women who have contributed their experience and ideas in these interviews, are all more than usually successful. Some have achieved distinction and eminence, a few are in positions of power and influence, all are pursuing their chosen careers with dedication and a high record of achievement. At the same time, they consider their families as being of greatest importance in their lives and set themselves high standards of personal integrity when allocating their priorities.

Most make light of natural endowments when asked to give reasons for their success. Instead, attention is focused on the support of a husband or the encouragement of parents, or simply on luck. Characteristic of all is the fact that they find nothing rare or special in their achievement, believing in a right for everyone to direct gifts of intellect, organizing skill and creative thought into worthwhile channels.

It is not surprising that husbands play a role of paramount importance in terms of providing encouragement and support. Less expected is the frequent mention of the influence of parents, even grandparents, in setting examples and implanting feelings of self-esteem.

There seem to be certain shared circumstances that contribute to the successful dovetailing of work and family life. For example, a husband who is successful in his own right – which these husbands tend to be – can support his wife financially during the years when she is building up a career and is not likely to experience feelings of rivalry when she achieves success. Some sharing of professional interests (although not necessarily in identical occupations) is an additional benefit which happens in two out of three cases. Many problems are avoided when marriage is seen as an active partnership in which each caters for the needs of the other – the husband by supporting his wife's aspirations, the wife by giving precedence to her husband's needs, in particular his career, when necessary. Much careful thought has been given to the implications of this last point.

A high degree of conscientiousness is common to all. On the domestic front, arrangements for looking after their children when young, which most of these women have had to make, are never left to chance. Helpers are carefully chosen and well rewarded. And however busy, mothers make sure that their children's everyday needs are met, from baking special cakes for a birthday party to buying spare parts for bicycles. This kind of involvement is seen as a continuing process; indeed, as their children grow up and their own parents age, finding surrogate care is considered increasingly inappropriate. Not one of these women thinks of such claims on her time as anything but natural and desirable.

Personal and public lives appear to reinforce each other: the consensus is that family life enhances work and perhaps even gives women the advantage of greater perspective and insight. Happy to accept their feminine role, some women claim qualities of compassion and skill in personal relationships as peculiarly feminine ones which help them in their work. When the demands of career and family are seen to conflict, choices are carefully considered and the consequences accepted. A minority chose to give up for some time; a number temporarily reduced their ambition; some changed careers, others deliberately postponed having children in order to establish themselves. But even the few who stopped work for an extended period, never ceased to build up work experience of some kind.

Long hours are accepted as an inevitable corollary of success. The adaptation to the requirements of family life is more easily made when some control can be exercised over the distribution of hours worked; this tends to be the case in senior positions and among the self-employed, the categories to which these women belong.

Being successful themselves, all readily assume that other women, including their own daughters, should be free to realize their potential. This does not mean that difficulties were not recognized or that criticism of existing attitudes was lacking. It was felt that women should reappraise their view of themselves, and that they should be given much more encouragement and practical help from outside. Those women who had had to stay at work throughout their careers in order not to jeopardize their chances of gaining experience and promotion, were critical of outmoded and inflexible attitudes. Some deplored the arbitrary emphasis on age and the rigidity among employers that has so far prevented many women from acquiring the learning and skills vital to their careers but not always made available at periods when they could be fitted in with family responsibilities. Some pointed out that women are too easily seen as being unreliable because of their legitimate priorities. They also felt that some women give up too easily. While one or two admitted that their ambition to reach the top had been curtailed by a wish to compromise for the sake of harmony and acceptance, others felt that they had been unnecessarily held back by outmoded custom. Recognizing that, in general, men care more about status and have a greater need to achieve through work, they nevertheless thought that the top positions – chairman of the board, chief editor, college president – should not always be reserved for men. A more equal share of the commanding heights was considered desirable as well as inevitable.

By way of a coda, a number of husbands contributed their own appraisal of their wives' qualities, the effects of her success on the life of the family, and their views about the future representation of the sexes in top jobs. Their answers – only occasionally less than serious – generally welcomed the benefits of having a successful wife and made light of the drawbacks. But, unlike the wives themselves, these husbands did not regard their partners' achievements as less than extraordinary, nor were they uniformly optimistic about the likelihood of large numbers of women following their example.

Nina Bawden received me in an airy study overlooking the garden, where she was working on her latest novel, Afternoon of a Good Woman. *Attractive and elegant, with a quick sense of humour and a lively response, she looked strikingly composed in her long, full skirt, even at this early hour of the day.*

What is most important in your life?

It varies from day to day, naturally. Work really, I suppose, with the family panting close behind. There are occasions when the family is more important – family crises. Some people's lives are more booby-trapped than others. Not all, of course, admit it.

How has this affected your career?

I would probably have written different sorts of books if I had had more leisure. But I have arranged my life so that I have enough time to write. When the children were small, time was more cramped. But you are never free – until you die. If it is not the children, there are aged parents. I have a friend who is more ruthless about her family, but she is also very lonely.

For the sort of books that I write, family trials are actually helpful. It is a pity to waste experiences. I have a small literary computer in a corner of my mind and have found good raw material in court and hospital waiting-rooms. It makes life more bearable. Work can be an escape.

How have you achieved success in your career?

Hard work and a bit of talent. I have worked very hard, probably harder than some others who wanted to write were prepared to do. I have been fairly ruthless, always working when I was not looking after babies, rarely shopping and never going out to morning coffee or lunch. All the spare time I had, I worked. This is what I wanted to do and what I liked doing best. I don't feel I gave up anything of importance. Some of my contemporaries who have not been as successful were probably not as obsessional about work.

The trouble with my job is that success makes one less secure, not more. If a couple of books are well received, one wants to go on getting better. If a book comes off, is well received critically and the next one is more difficult or perhaps not so good, one worries. It all depends on how ambitious you are. In a way success is slightly alarming. The standard is always higher. The possibilities are limitless. A lot of writing, though, is knowing one's limitations and working round them.

How do you manage home and a career?

I have been very fortunate. My career has worked in very well. For years, when I couldn't have supported myself by writing, I was kept by my husband – kept, fed, allowed to have babies and do a job, too. A lot of women underestimate this sort of luxury which not many other societies provide.

I wrote my first novel when my older son was four and my second son one year old. Creatively it worked rather well. I wrote whenever I could, when children were sleeping or taken out for a walk, and I used the time fully. I find present problems of telephones and seeing to the gutters more irritating than small children's demands. A male novelist would be protected by his wife. In fact, if one is a successful writer it is better to be a man. I would like a little wife now to take some of the burdens off.

Older children are more draining. We have five in and out of the house, all with their separate demands and problems, and one can no longer play a game with them and put them to bed. The disadvantage of working at home is that you are always left with the sick aunt and the weeping adolescent. It's your kitchen they are sitting in. Your husband meanwhile is on the 8-o'clock train.

The old are much worse in a way, difficult in a different way. There is the changing-over of roles with one's parents. They become your children just at the point when your own are acting up. And you can't share these difficulties with your own parents. Our generation is trapped; we were conditioned to think that our children's problems were our fault. Our parents, free from this sort of guilt, can sit and condemn them. We stand like an Aunt Sally between them both, protecting old parents from the worst of the children's doings – and the children from their disapproval. By this I mean anything in the area of long hair, drugs, sex – not what is necessarily, in itself, bad. There has been such an enormous change in social and sexual attitudes since our parents were young that they find our children's customs hard to grasp. The elderly are potential disaster areas.

If I had had no children my books would have been quite different. They are about inter-personal relations, and it is in the home that passions run highest. It is the only place people have a real theatrical life.

I can't imagine just being a 'mum', though. I should probably have been more managing and bossy. Where would all that energy have gone? It might have been more, or less, tiresome for the children. I would have mended more clothes, but interfered more in their lives.

Why do you think there are so few women at the top, and what about the future?

I think that the women who would be at the top now are our generation who were handicapped in two ways. Bowlby and Spock and the importance of the mother-and-child relationship, *and* the special pressures to bear children which are always present in any society after a war. I think social attitudes take a long time to change – for changes to filter through from the intellect to the emotions, anyway – and it is only very recently that young women of the kind likely to reach the 'top' have begun to decide, consciously, not to have children. (On the other hand I do wonder how much children really handicap a determined woman? Perhaps it isn't children so much as husbands that are a handicap?) Those who do are more willing to leave them, less inhibited than we were, now that they know it makes no difference. We will not know the effect of these changes for twenty years.

HUSBAND'S COMMENTS

Can you single out any special qualities possessed by your wife which have enabled her to successfully combine family life with a demanding career?

A ruthless determination to pursue singlemindedly her vocation and not to be subdued by social and sexual systems and imposed rules; the good fortune to possess a talent which was at once both creatively satisfying and capable of being developed and evolved at home, while having a respectable capacity for earning money. In short, talent, dedication and an ability to work very hard.

What effect, would you say, has your wife's professional involvement had on your life as a family?

Most enriching, enlivening and certainly restoring in balancing the distorted Mum/Dad stereotypes. There have been minor disadvantages for the weaker members of a family somewhat boisterous with over-performers. But the same could, with equal justice, be said of me.

In the light of your experience at home (and professionally) do you think it is realistic to expect an increase in the number of women who will put themselves forward to fill positions of high responsibility in the future?

Yes – to put themselves forward, or so I most profoundly believe and hope.

I am less certain as to the achieving of such a significant increase. Why? I suspect because for most wives and mothers to succeed they need an extra dollop of dedication, self-discipline and great strength of purpose. And there aren't many willing to be as determined and hard-working as all that. Not many men, either.

ANNE BELOFF-CHAIN

BIOCHEMIST AND READER, LONDON UNIVERSITY

Dr Beloff-Chain's (Lady Chain's) office is a modest oasis of comfort and quiet amid the hum of computers and the clatters and odours of the myriad of laboratories that surround it. A roughcast model of an Irish croft, executed by her youngest son many years ago, sits on a vast metal filing cabinet outside the door: inside, a gallery of snapshots and portraits of jolly children faces a clinical photograph of mice, much enlarged. But you notice first on the wall the wise and humorous face of her husband. Her manner is warm and relaxed, her appearance handsome in a comfortable way.

Can you say what is most important in your life?

Without any hesitation, my family, by which I mean my husband and my three children. I have been lucky in my career because my husband and I have been able to work together. But I am emphatically not Women's Lib : I do not feel that it is necessary to have a career because you have a brain. One's career is so much a matter of luck : what is most important of all is how one's husband feels about it. I hold no theories and have no passion about the career question; the role of chance is so tremendous and choices so individual.

How have you managed at home?

Again, I have been terribly lucky. We spent the first fifteen years bringing up our children in Italy where help was easy. I found a marvellous experienced Italian nanny who came back to England with us and is now our housekeeper. Our children have not been deprived in any way. The Italian custom of a long lunch and afternoon break was a great advantage too : I made a point of spending the afternoons with the children as well as the weekends, and went back to work in the evenings. Nowadays it is almost impossible to find such a person as our nanny: without her competence and reliability my career would have been impossible. I would not have been prepared to leave my children otherwise. Temporary and *au pair* arrangements are not the same. And there is such a lot to do even if you do have help.

What are the problems?

It is an exhausting kind of life, even with help. You shouldn't do it unless you are blessed with stamina, energy and health: all of which I have. I would not advise a young woman to do the same. Many people can live happily without having a career outside the home, they can develop their interests in the home. I am not 100 per cent happy with the way I live. I often feel I want more time for myself: I am never on my own: one gives up a lot. Also one does get more tired as one gets older and there is a feeling of pressure all the time. Experimental science is intellectually demanding – I think there are many careers easier than science. For instance, in some other jobs you can give up for a time, like teaching, and have school holidays. I went back to work very soon after my babies were born, never really had a break at all. This was essential because one would get out of touch so quickly and one cannot be part-time. Experimental science really is not suitable for a woman, unless she has a strong motivation.

Can you say how you have achieved success in your career?

I have not been as successful as I might have been. There is no question about that. But I decided when we started our family that I was not going to do some of the time-consuming things one must do if one is seeking advancement. To make oneself well known one must travel, attend meetings and give papers. But I made the conscious decision that I would concentrate on my family. I have always thought children were more important than my career.

I have always been hard-working and conscientious. My mother's influence is important: she was extraordinarily intelligent, both feminist and intellectual. She may have felt she missed out by not having a career although she devoted her life to her family and originated valuable welfare schemes which I work for myself today. She read law at Leningrad University which was rare enough for a woman but considered impossible for a Jew. She was determined that her daughters should have careers. But I do not feel the same way about my daughter, not at all.

I was well into my career when I married at twenty-seven, by which time I had spent two years doing research at Harvard Medical School in the US. But I did not postpone marriage for career reasons, I just hadn't met the right person. Biochemistry was not taught at university when I was an undergraduate. I read chemistry and then sought advice from a scientist who was an old friend of the family and whom I subsequently married. He suggested biochemistry.

My own life is an example of what I mean when I say chance is important at every turn. We met frequently in the years 1942-1945 when I was working for a Ph.D. degree in the Biochemistry Department at Oxford, and he was working on penicillin at the William Dunn School of Pathology. The war made it more natural to marry late. We went to Italy because a remarkable personality in Rome offered my husband all the large-scale fermentation facilities he wanted for his researches into antibiotics and the substances produced by micro organisms, which he was unable to get in England. So many crucial decisions and successful enterprises depend on individuals, not committees. I was able (by chance not by plan) to help him with the new set-up. Consequently, we waited six years to have children.

My work, which I now find exciting, has arisen through my original interest in the mechanism of insulin action and diabetes. I am trying to find out what is the primary defect in a breed of genetically obese mice, of which we have a breeding colony. A recessive gene produces obesity in which a high insulin level develops in the blood, but due to an insulin resistance they are unable to metabolize glucose normally. In this way these animals have an abnormal glucose tolerance curve and other characteristics which in many respects resemble the clinical condition known as 'maturity onset diabetes', which is frequently associated with obesity.

But I would be prepared to give up my experimental work

tomorrow in order to get involved in the politics of education, if I thought I could become influential. I haven't given the fact that there are very few women in decision-taking positions much thought, but it does aggravate me that not a single college head in this university is a woman.

I feel strongly that there must be an elite in education and that the notion that practically everyone should go to university is a nonsense. I can't think why so many employers say they want graduates. They would be much better off with an intake of seventeen- to eighteen-year-olds and providing more in-training. The aims of education seem to have got out of balance : a combination of technical skills and general education is the best preparation for life for most people, and pride in doing something with one's hands is important. We have created a false snobbishness about universities. But as long as grants to departments depend on numbers, universities are bound to go on trying to attract more students. Entrance standards in the sciences are far too low in many universities and we don't need more mediocre scientists. I don't believe any more that party politics can effect change and committees who make the important decisions about higher education are self-perpetuating : they always choose the people who won't go against the stream. I would like to get involved but I think it is too late.

Are there advantages in being a woman in your profession?

No.

Disadvantages?

It is entirely a matter of available time. There is no prejudice in experimental science, you just have to do good work. The administration and politics of science is another matter. There are few full professors or heads of departments who are women.

Do women disadvantage themselves?

Only in the sense that they may give less time to their job because of home life. On the contrary, because women have to be particularly well motivated to be doing it at all, they are on the whole rather good at their work.

To what extent are external factors to blame for the lack of women at the top?

The situation has undoubtedly got worse but I am at a loss to explain it. It may be that women marry more, and younger. But I don't give much thought to the special position of women working. I would not be inclined to blame schools: it is not necessary to have sophisticated laboratory equipment to become involved in science, although the quality of the teaching is of course important. The outstanding and really motivated ones will make up later anyhow.

What can be done to improve the career position of women?

If they really want to be scientists, they will be. It is very difficult to combine experimental scientific work with family life, as I have said and I think that many of the women who take a science degree should be encouraged to teach; we need more good science teachers.

What advice would you give to girls who want to have children and a satisfying career?

The subject you study at school and later should interest you: only a few need to know where they are going. The rest need time to mature. They will find ways of filling their time if they have enough interests. I prefer not to generalize: it is such an individual matter and luck plays such a large part.

Can you sum up the advantages and disadvantages of combining a family and career in your own life?

As I have already said, I don't have enough time for myself and I haven't had time to cultivate a hobby. I was a keen tennis player until I had a family, but after that found little time for it. Relaxation is essential in such a busy and hectic life. We have found it on the West coast of Ireland. We have built ourselves a house there: we did everything locally and we adore it.

What changes would you like to see in the future?

Science teaching at the university should be run for a few carefully selected scientists. I do think everyone at the university, whatever course they are taking, should learn some basic science and something about scientific methods. This is one of the concepts which will be introduced at the University College of Buckingham, the first Independent University in this country, in which I was involved first on the Planning Committee and now on the Academic Council.

We don't teach enough about how to use leisure; so many of the problems today are due to people being bored.

HUSBAND'S COMMENTS

Can you single out any special qualities possessed by your wife which have enabled her to successfully combine family life with a demanding career?

She has an unusual talent for organization, both in the laboratory in relation to her staff and the department as a whole, and at home, bringing up the children and looking after our extensive social engagements. The availability of an efficient housekeeper from the time of birth of our children until the present was a considerable help.

What effect, would you say, has your wife's professional involvement had on your life as a family?

As my wife and I have the same profession, worked in the same institute and therefore saw each other frequently during the day, we could forget our daily experiences with regard to work the moment we returned home and could concentrate on the children. This strengthened our family ties.

In the light of your experience at home (and professionally) do you think it is realistic to expect an increase in the number of women who will put themselves forward to fill positions of high responsibility in the future?

My own experience has shown that women can be excellent organizers. In addition I believe women in western society have many character qualities men do not possess, making them eminently suited for occupying successfully important positions of responsibility both in political and social life, as well as in administration. As opportunities arise, women will be eager to fill such posts.

*Marion Boyars, who owns and runs a lively and successful pub-
lishing firm bearing her name, delights in not only being a
woman, but a small woman. She is informal in appearance and
manner, with a great sense of fun and a ready laugh. She seems
at ease and confident in any company, tackling questions and
problems in a thoughtful and decisive way. Her daughters, aged
twenty and eighteen, are both studying away from home and she
lives with her second husband in a mews house overflowing with
books, magazines, pictures and records.*

What is most important in your life?

The most important things to me are certain qualities : integrity –
being true to myself, and loyalty – being true to others. By
integrity I do not mean a kind of prissy purity, but a wholeness
of personality, an awareness of strengths and weaknesses, a willingness to admit to these and to correct oneself. It is something
to live up to, an ideal, and it involves a severe honesty which is
not necessarily comfortable to live with. If one is able to achieve
this, and recognize it in others, one is more capable of giving.
What I aim for in myself and admire in others is a constant working on oneself, yielding to instinct but at the same time analysing
one's values and practising what one professes to believe in.
Priorities are, I think, a mixture of who needs one most and
where one cannot be replaced. But one must not be burdensome
if it turns out that one's assessment of others' needs may have
been mistaken. For example, when the children were small they
needed me physically more than a business associate might; now
that they are older they need me more as a counsellor or someone
who is just naturally more interested than other people in their
problems. In case of conflict choice should ideally be dictated by

a concern for others, and I think this is on the whole more likely where one has an inner strength and security.

I think I have been quite a successful mother – my children can stand on their own feet. Apart from my children, my husband and my job, friends also have a high priority. My friends are very important to me and if a friend needs me I'll drop everything.

How do you manage at home?

In the early days I was fortunate to have enough money : I could afford a full-time nanny. When the children were small they never noticed that I went to work – they thought I was going shopping. The nanny stayed for a long time. She looked after the flat and did everything except cook. I've always loved cooking and done it whenever I was at home. I don't consider myself a very sophisticated cook but I'm very interested in food and I take care over what I prepare. I don't like delegating cooking – I enjoy it too much. But I have no particular ambition to be a good housewife – I'm not at all highly organized in the house. Now that we don't need living-in help any more, I have a cleaner three hours a week. And we have a dishwasher which has cut my clean-ing bills – no messy kitchen. I hate mess. Since my husband works from home he creates more of a mess than I do, but we actually run the house together and have no conflicts about that. He does most of the daily shopping and cares about prices. We have a smooth routine for entertaining : he sets the table, looks after the wine, cheese and coffee, and I do the cooking and serving. We follow this for ourselves as well. We literally do everything together.

What are the problems?

There aren't many. Not now. The problem of time allocation was real when the children were small. My husband and I share intellectual interests and my publishing is of the kind where his immense knowledge is useful and much appreciated. But his interests are for enjoyment, mine are translated into a professional activity. He understands that. He is very well liked by the girls, amuses them and stretches their minds. It was more difficult when they were small because he had no interest in entering into their minds, and not being their real father found some of my caring incomprehensible. If there are any conflicts, it is that he is a demanding husband who wants my physical presence a lot while I have to be involved with so many things and people. Also, my biggest problem is that I have no space for myself – for working at home or just being alone. A five-bedroomed house should give me that space, but my husband is a magpie collector and the children are following suit!

Can you say how you achieved success in your career?

Luck. I was lucky in my background (school and university in four countries), and in choosing a career that was right for me. I first came to publishing through answering an advertisement – someone was looking for a partner. I had two small children and no publishing experience. Or no direct experience. But my father was a publisher and though he never thought of himself as very successful, he was a publisher through and through. He was my knight in shining armour, very handsome and imposing. Once I was a publisher I had to learn fast and I had to work to make a success of it. I think that I'm a gifted publisher, with intellectual curiosity and a practical bent. Other people find me dedicated – I suppose they're right. Publishing is an activity and not a job.

Are there advantages in being a woman in your profession?

Certainly. There are advantages not only in being a woman but in being a small woman. Businessmen are not as tough with women as they are with other men. When I deal with men I'm always conscious of being a woman, of interacting as a woman with a man. As an editor I give authors (men and women) confidence because I don't try to put forward my own ideas against theirs – I do what is best for the book. I try to put myself in the background and it works better – this is true of most women, I think. The Women's Lib Movement has helped women enormously. Women don't envy each other as they used to – now it's recognition rather than envy. I like intelligent, successful women – I find them interesting and rewarding and I don't envy them. Another advantage is that women are more patient than men – they allow things to develop.

Are there any disadvantages?

The same patience can be a disadvantage; one doesn't always act when one ought to. Also, there are real disadvantages sometimes in being a woman dealing with men. Relationships can be very close and complex in this profession. Some men can't bear being told what to do by a woman. Or they don't listen very carefully to what a woman says – it must be the voice. I think the male voice carries more authority. If they won't listen to you you have to assert yourself in an indirect way. I consider that *they* have the problem – I don't. I can't change my sex, I just try to carry on and ignore the fact that they are really discriminating against me. The other thing is that if a woman wants to succeed she has to be much better than a man and work much harder. An average kind of woman can't get to the top the way an average man can.

Do women disadvantage themselves?

Enormously. By not having enough confidence. The Women's Movement has given women a modicum of confidence, but not half enough. I think women are going about it the wrong way. They shouldn't make demands. You can't fight the establishment by head-on screaming. The heightened consciousness and sense of security and achievement will take the stigma out of ambition for women which is still regarded as a character defect – by men *and* women. Women are less willing to take responsibility. I find this particularly when I try to employ people. Men do this much more readily, even if their abilities aren't greater. Again, women often don't apply for the top jobs, probably because of lack of confidence.

To what extent are outside circumstances to blame for the lack of women at the top?

All the way through. It begins with education. Society imposes certain ideas on children – in a girl's case that she has to please. That's why girls often do better at school than boys – they like to please their teachers. Later their performance drops – they're trying to please their boy-friends or lovers. Expectations for women are pitched too low and this puts women at a disadvantage – it undermines their confidence from the beginning. The same low expectations also produce all the usual prejudices: women aren't as reliable as men, they don't take their jobs as seriously, etc. Women subscribe to these as much as men do. The psychological disabilities are the main enemy – once these have been surmounted and shed (by both men and women), laws, customs and opportunities will follow.

What can be done to improve the career position of women?

Women must gain in consciousness and confidence. This will have its effect right through society. In that sense the Women's Movement is very important. The Anti-Discrimination Bill is an enormously important beginning. At present women are barred from certain jobs and there are quotas in some professions (e.g. medicine and university teaching) – at least as far as admission and training are concerned. Later there are other barriers – there aren't many women in publishing or law. The trade unions are still very retrograde – male-oriented and prejudiced. In printing, women aren't allowed near machinery, which may be justified because some of it is heavy; but they aren't allowed to be compositors either, and they'd be good at that. Perhaps after the Bill is passed we'll see more women in middle or top managing positions. Only weak men fear able women. (They also fear able men, but less so.)

Have you any advice to give to girls who want to have children and a satisfying career?

Do it. And help to bring about change and a sense of greater equality: in the image of yourself and in the image of marriage. Prepare and conduct your marriage with as much care as your career. If you fall for a very traditional and hide-bound male, don't hope to change him: don't marry him.

What changes would you like to see in the future?

Increased self-confidence among women. Also, the institutions of marriage and parenthood must be re-examined: we should get rid of double-standards for men and women. Marriage should be thought of as a partnership and not as a special career for a girl. In the same way, living together and sex before and in marriage should be reconsidered. The prejudice shouldn't be against the woman. Women have labels attached to them to their disadvantage – they should be got rid of once and for all. Labels attached to people (both men and women) are irrational, counter-productive and stifling. The establishment and the status quo have landed us in the present difficulties. We need all the talent we can muster. We can well do without the rituals which a male-dominated society has imposed on us: rules of procedure, submission to pride and vanity, clubland, the old school tie, organized hypocrisy, etc. Women should not ape these but point out how ridiculous they are. Since women have less of a vested interest in political and economic institutions, they are in a position to supply original and revolutionary ideas. But women's ambitions and abilities should not coddle men into laziness and idleness (there is a real danger that this is happening).

What advantages have you found in having both a career and a family?

A very full life. I have had everything and I wouldn't have wanted to miss any of it. When one is fully occupied and is excited and stimulated, it keeps the adrenalin flowing. One can do things. The ups and downs, the real pleasures and the real pains have made me into a whole person living in a real world.

Any disadvantages?

Not really, except time is always a problem. One has to make quick decisions and they aren't always the right ones.

HUSBAND'S COMMENTS

Can you single out any special qualities possessed by your wife which have enabled her to successfully combine family life with a demanding career?

Her enthusiasm. She *chose* her profession and has done what she wanted with her life.

What effect, would you say, has your wife's professional involvement had on your life as a family?

Her professional life has never interfered with family life. The girls have always fully accepted it – from the time they understood what she was doing – and nobody has got steamed up, except Marion perhaps. One might say that our social life has been enriched.

In the light of your experience at home (and professionally) do you think it is realistic to expect an increase in the number of women who will put themselves forward to fill positions of high responsibility in the future?

Yes.

C

SANTA RAYMOND BURRILL

ARCHITECT IN PRIVATE PRACTICE

Santa Burrill has large intense eyes in a fine face, and there is glamour in her self-confidence. She works to promote the cause of women professionals, especially in her own profession. She was interviewed in hospital where she was awaiting the birth of her third child, in a bed strewn with architectural drawings.

What is most important in your life?

My husband, then my children aged two and four, and then my work.

How do you manage at home and how have you managed in the past?

I have a young trained person to look after the children. My husband would have employed a nanny anyway because he wants to see the children when he feels like it and not otherwise. I try to save one day a week to spend with the children. I love them very much but I honestly find them exhausting and also boring if I am with them all the time. The domestic chores bore me too. I try to have high-powered help: don't ask me how to find it, but of course one must pay well. I am sure my children are better off with someone who has more patience than I do. But it is important for me to remain integral to their lives, and I do see them every day.

What are the problems?

My husband's attitude is vital and I am constantly aware of the danger of alienation. He needs nurturing and 'servicing', otherwise he is deprived and cannot do his work properly. We were

66

both brought up to believe that looking after her husband is a woman's most important job, and I don't think that idea is changing much. However, I have always thought that men fall into two categories : those who like having a working wife and don't mind working for a woman, and those who are the opposite. I think it is a fact of life that at the end of the working day it is the husband who must be allowed to moan while the wife must put on a cheerful face and get on with the supper. Otherwise there is no conflict and I am one of those who must be happy at home in order to work outside. I admit that a few people actually work better when they are unhappy, but I am not one of them.

Can you say how you achieved success in your career?

My parents were both 'doers' and encouraged me; that makes a huge difference. I married at thirty after having lots of practical work experience. Early influences are terribly important : my mother had worked and my parents expected me to become self-supporting. I might have become an artist or designer instead of an architect, which I became slightly by accident. I was a late developer : at polytechnic I did badly for a year or two although I enjoyed the work. Then suddenly things fell into place and I did some drawings in my third year that I am still proud of. I went after the professional qualification because I knew it would be difficult and it was a challenge to me. I know that my work is consistently of good standard which gives me keen pleasure, but I would not call myself ambitious. I mind about small things that make life better and easier for people. It is too early for me to claim to be successful : my children are still very young; ask me in ten years' time. I hope I am being successful in keeping a career going. Whilst one is having children one can only expect to keep one's value up; one cannot expect to make money or carry great responsibility.

Are there advantages in being a woman in your profession?

It's about fifty-fifty. If you behave like a woman it's a case of swings and roundabouts. In my profession one can score by being helpless, looking a little foolish, not minding losing face, asking

advice, using womanly wiles, smoothing troubled waters. I work
from the basis that men and women are quite different – bio-
logically. But equal. If both learn to exploit their strength, that's
fine. Many women now tend to act like second-class men. It's
easier for the average man to deal with a woman who looks like
one; that's why I always dress like one, wear skirts to work. I
believe women in my profession can be very good. Women can
be very good designers while keeping in touch with practicalities.
It is possible to reduce working hours to fit in with other demands,
such as the work intensity of one's husband, and to make free
time for one's husband as well as for children. But one must have
put in a lot of full-time experience first: most young architects
work in local authorities and this is where women can find most
part-time work.

Are there disadvantages?

One can easily become exhausted by overwork. I have found
very few disadvantages and never come up against discrimination,
although women architects older than myself have. Local authority employers don't distinguish between the sexes: private firms
are more likely to take sex into account. One does ask oneself why
there are so few creative women about apart from novelists. Is it
that they spend their creativity having babies, or is it all the
interruptions like having to cook dinner?

Do women disadvantage themselves?

Yes, by being unreliable, and sometimes by expecting to be
treated badly. Also, they are probably less singleminded than
men, more affected by outside factors like an unhappy love affair.
Some women are totally reliable, whatever situation they find
themselves in. Many others are not. One hears of women persuad-
ing employers to give them responsible jobs, then letting them
down. Women are their own worst enemies. I don't blame the
world for *not* putting women in positions of responsibility.
Women use the excuse of having to go with their husbands, not
the other way round.

What can be done to improve the career position of women?

Women at the top seem to be either unmarried, divorced or elderly. There won't be many at the top until women stop having their cake and eating it. It's fundamental. To be, and stay, at the top we have to know that we can't really opt out, go back to being the little woman at the sink. There will be no change until we are all totally committed.

What advice would you give to girls who want to have a family and a satisfying career?

The most important thing is *not* to stop. You must go on working, even if very little, say one hour a day. It needn't be in your own field, it can be unpaid social work. It is important to keep your mind and your whole attitude to work alive. After a gap women become rusty, unprofessional, lacking in self-confidence. It's difficult to get going again once you've stopped. The ladder structure is difficult; it should be much easier to get back on. If you are not working, time at home gets spun out with unnecessary activities. A friend whom I told that I was only working very little wisely remarked : 'Ah, you're working; that is itself an investment.' In this way you keep your value on the open market. One must get one's husband and children accustomed to the fact that one is working. Children at an early age get used to having other people around. There are ways of getting the children looked after, such as swopping systems. Getting more courses for women, especially refresher courses, is also important, but this is not a simple issue. (Ann Ackland of the Architectural Association ran one but not many people attended and these did not find it any easier to get jobs as a result.)

What changes would you like to see?

Where possible, husband and wife should share non-working tasks; this should be so right across the social scale. I'm not a Women's Libber. One great problem is that many women take and don't give anything in return. They are brought up to expect a man to go out and earn for them, spend their time drinking coffee and having their hair done. It is a frightful thought that a man is forced to work from nine to five to earn a living for his family. Until there is more equality here, there can't be more in terms of opportunities for women. In many ways the world is biased against men. It is also true that employers' attitudes must be changed. They have got to meet women half-way, allow more erratic, flexible hours and less work in school holidays. They have got to see women as part of the organization, reckon to use them. This is tricky in the current financial climate where there are many able men unable to find work. But there must be more acceptance that women go out to work. In the rat race of today you have to go pretty hard not to slide downhill. Even a five-year break will make you lag behind your colleagues coming up.

What I would like to see change the most are female attitudes, a greater commitment to work. And another thing; some girls do enjoy domestic science and could be encouraged to work professionally with children and in the home as equals with the mother who chooses to work outside.

What advantages or disadvantages have you found in having a career and a family?

Shirley Conran's point that you can have a husband, children and a job but not all three at the same time is to some extent true. The current climate that assigns fixed roles to men and women (that he should concern himself with money matters; that she should 'service' her husband) doesn't help. There are enormous disadvantages in trying to do all three things well. I find it incredibly difficult and exhausting. I'm not very strong physically and get very tired and bad-tempered. I like to look pretty, to cook good food, to entertain my husband's friends, to go out with my husband (he's a social animal), to be a companion to him and spend time with the children. (I don't believe they need as much as one might think, but probably more than one can ever give them.) It's a question of caring for their mental and physical welfare, doing things with them, loving them, teaching them, playing with them, making sure they get what they need from life, keeping an eye on them and the people who look after them. Then there are the demands of work : trying to do a good job, helping others working for one to do the same and to enjoy their work. It's very difficult to do three well; one always feels 'oh dear!'

Work makes me a more interesting person. I'm idle by nature and if I didn't work I would sit and do nothing much. My job keeps my mind active in all fields. I am a more lively person for my husband. Though he gets upset at my overdoing it, he's very interested. From the children's point of view – long-term – I have more to contribute, am off their backs and not likely to rely on them for emotional stability. I have my own thing and it's nice to earn money. I sometimes wonder what the difference is between trying to build up a career and just 'working'. I suppose it goes back to trying to build something up, to responsibility, thinking long-term, not just being a mother. It is difficult for working mothers to maintain the necessary continuity. I never thought that life was just for getting married. My parents thought I should work, be self-supporting and do something worthwhile.

HUSBAND'S COMMENTS

Can you single out any special qualities possessed by your wife which have enabled her to successfully combine family life with a demanding career?

A power of concentration. Santa can work successfully with the children around her, something I find impossible.

What effect, would you say, has your wife's professional involvement had on your life as a family?

Very little, since Santa invariably works in with my demanding schedules, particularly holidays, evenings out and so on.

In the light of your experience at home (and professionally) do you think it is realistic to expect an increase in the number of women who will put themselves forward to fill positions of high responsibility in the future?

I would hope so – I enjoy working for women.

SUSAN BARNES CROSLAND

BIOGRAPHER AND JOURNALIST

(The meetings with Mrs Crosland took place during the summer of 1976. Her husband, the Rt. Hon. Anthony Crosland, MP, died at the Radcliffe Infirmary, Oxford, on 12 February, 1977.)

Susan Crosland's fair hair was tied back with a scarf, her athletic figure dressed in a pretty sprigged cotton. Direct and friendly, but with a certain hesitant shyness that would make a stranger tread warily, she is an endearingly private person. Her high-ceilinged drawing-room, hung with pictures in challenging variety, is at once colourful and comfortable, and the view high over the gardens below is a marvel in the heart of the city. The intermittent wail of the Siamese cat was invariably silenced by a bounce to open the door to permit entry and exit in turn.

Can you say what is most important in your life?

Family, now and always. That is, two daughters who are grown up now – one is married and the other is twenty-one and independent, of course. They have always been my paramount concern, especially while they were growing up. And my husband Tony.

How do you manage at home now, and how did you manage then?

When the children were little I employed a mother's help – the cost was not prohibitive in those days, and I needed to go out to work to support the family. (Also, by then I *wanted* to have an outside job.) She stayed for years : she was Italian and had friends of her own, which was essential so that she didn't expect companionship of me. Eventually she decided that she was leading too vicarious a life and returned to Italy; but we understood each other and I didn't need her so much by then. When the children were older I managed with an *au pair* combined with some daily cleaning help. The children learned to take buses from an early

73

age: fortunately we lived on a bus route direct to school. It may seem a funny thing to say, but my children were brought up to be well behaved and so I could take them anywhere with me.

When they were in their middle teens and an *au pair* could no longer be expected to act *in loco parentis*, I gave up having one and instead had more help from the invaluable daily. When I went away on trips with my husband, a friend's aunt – who herself became a close friend – moved in to do the *in loco parentis* bit.

Having said how well behaved the children were, I have to admit that I was caught totally unprepared for the horrors of adolescence. I reckon it lasts about three years. That made a total of six years for us. Through those times my husband's moral support was indispensable.

In the days when I had to work full-time – before I remarried – I was permitted to work a five-day-week in four days. I had an understanding editor and I managed my time very differently from my male colleagues: when it was pointed out to me that I was amazingly well organized, I was surprised; I just did what suited me – which was to skip socializing with my colleagues and instead take sandwiches to eat at my desk so that I could write letters and figure out the plumber's bills and so on and get domestic chores done as far as possible in the midday break. I was always determined to leave myself free for the children when I got home from work – and free to go out if I felt like it in the evening.

I gave up full-time work and freelanced from home when I remarried. From everyone's point of view it was essential that I be based at home. My children were by then adolescents and at the local comprehensive school and needed supervision. We have not been 'permissive' parents. And my husband was working these incredible politicians' hours. The only thing to be said for these ungodly hours is that we didn't all arrive home at the same time of day dead tired and I didn't have the problem of splitting time between my husband and the kids: I could concentrate on each in turn. If necessary I would go to bed and set the alarm for Tony's return.

I used to be gregarious but am less so now. Last year we bought a country cottage – about the last of our colleagues to do so. But we'd finally decided that we do need to get away. Occasionally our London home has been besieged, either by journalists or by political demonstrators. We happened to see a mill house when we were visiting the Crossmans several years ago and fell for it, and when it came onto the market later on, it seemed like fate. I suspect that the country cottage would have created problems when the children were adolescent because it would have complicated all our lives : I would not have been prepared to leave them in town on their own, for instance.

For the last six years my helper has been Eileen. She comes in the mornings and can do anything. In fact she is a butler *manqué* and likes nothing more than ushering in people who have come to see me for my work or to see Tony if he happens to be working at home. I do as much of my interviewing at home as possible. I sometimes think life would be unendurable without Eileen to battle with the front-door bell : she protects me.

What are the problems arising from your particular combination of professional and family life?

I suppose there are problems when you are married to a man who needs enormous backing. Inevitably there are times when your own pursuits must be abandoned. I have been lucky up to now. The jobs my husband previously held – at Education and at the Board of Trade and the Department of the Environment – have been enormously demanding of him but did not carry demanding jobs for me. I did go on his long trips – for instance I went three times to Russia – but I didn't have a great many lunches or dinners to cope with. I am thankful the children are grown up now. The frequent business of getting ready to go out, having to think about what you are going to put on and whom you are going to meet : it would have been very wearing if I had had to deal with the children as well. (Next week I must drop absolutely everything for the State Visit.)

There have been occasional moments of terrible pressure. I got exceedingly tired towards the end of four years in Opposition. Although it was a lovely time in many ways, with my husband working at home in the mornings and often home for lunch, people streamed through the house to see him and would often stay for a sandwich with us – and though I enjoyed (most of) these various activities there just were not enough hours to go round. I did not start out as a political creature, though my natural feelings were always leftish. My husband has developed and refined these feelings. But I remain more interested in politicians as individuals than in the details of policy – which suits my husband just as well! I think that the bit I find most difficult temperamentally in being a politician's wife is canvassing at election time – ringing doorbells and asking people to vote for him.

When we came back into Government in 1974, I had just completed for the *Sunday Times* a profile on Jeremy Thorpe which was also just in time to be included in the book of my profiles that Cape was publishing (*Behind the Image*). It seemed a good moment to take some time off – both to get some rest and to decide whether to go on with journalism or switch to another form of writing. I had imagined that I would use my year off to do leisurely and delightful things like spending time in the Reading Room at the British Museum and visiting art galleries regularly – but to my chagrin, a great lethargy overtook me. When you stop overworking, you wonder whether you will ever be able to do anything again. All work suddenly becomes an immense effort. Presumably it's a matter of your adrenalin disappearing when you let up. In a sense that lovely year off was wasted. The only thing to show for it is the country cottage which I eventually found and put together.

I can get in a panic about money, and we decided early on that I would pay my earnings over to my husband and he would then pay me a monthly 'allowance'. We keep separate bank accounts and obviously I deal with ordinary bills, but I leave my husband to grapple with the mortgage and overdrafts and so on.

Can you say how you achieved success in your career?

I have had more than one career. I began as a lecturer at the Baltimore Museum of Art. Teaching was not my vocation, but a strongly developed visual perspective on history remains terribly important to me. This was acquired at Vassar. I worked at the Museum until a few months before my first child was born.

In London eight years later, when my second child was five, I both wanted and had to have a job that paid well. I decided to try journalism. I brazened it out, going straight to the top man as one must, and was taken on as a features writer by the *Sunday Express*. I think it is easier to approach the top man with a partly feigned confidence if one is anonymous, as I then was. And it was a help to be foreign as this meant less than the usual inspection of credentials, which was just as well.

When I remarried, I left the *Sunday Express* and began freelancing under contract, first to the old *Sun*, then to the *Sunday Times*. I prefer working in my own time. I love dealing with facts – which I have always found more bizarre than fiction. In the last couple of years of writing 7,000-10,000 word profiles for the *Sunday Times*, I found I was doing enough research on some articles to write a short book. I would become terribly involved with the subject and invariably, by the time I had reached the final draft, there would be a slight 'frisson' in the household over the fact that with these piles of notes and drafts sitting along one wall and with my concentration on them, the subject appeared to have moved right into the home. Having said that, my husband is immensely helpful and encouraging and will concentrate his mind on my work when I seek his editorial advice. He is one of those husbands who think wives should work. But obviously, when he eventually gets home and brings with him immense amounts of work still to be done, I try not to present my own work problems to him as well.

Having decided to make the leap from journalism to biography, I wanted a subject who could combine my interest in the visual with my fascination in the creative tension of human beings. And I wanted to write about someone outside politics, despite the fact that I have always found politicians particularly fascinating to interview : some of them have a recklessness and indiscretion which I rarely found in interviewing a businessman, for instance. But increasingly, because of my husband's own position, I found writing political profiles was getting too near the bone. For years I have been interested in Jacob Epstein, and for some reason there is no biography of him, despite his being

Britain's most controversial sculptor in this century pre-Moore. So I have embarked on a biography of Epstein.

Are there advantages in being a woman in your profession?

Certainly there are in those forms of journalism where women are few and thus there is less competition. In my experience, women are more conscientious. Paradoxically, they are often more re-laxed about their 'careers' because they are many-sided. Also, women don't normally have the anxiety of being cut off from their work at retirement, because they always have domestic work to do; and I think they don't fear old age as much as men, for the same reason.

Are there disadvantages?

There are certain subjects I should have enjoyed working on which I have avoided on my husband's account. As I have said, I am endlessly fascinated by politicians and would enjoy writing about them. Is it their boldness that makes them so attractive?

Do you think that women disadvantage themselves?

I feel sure they do, but I'm afraid I haven't thought about it much.

There aren't many women at the top. To what extent do you think external factors are to blame?

I myself have never wanted to be an editor; I have not been ambitious in the sense of power-seeking. I am not at all sure whether this has been a matter of circumstance or whether it is my inborn nature.

My attitudes have been somewhat altered by being married to a public person. It has made me even more privatized – also, of course, I can be bruised vicariously. I am more philosophical than I used to be but it has made me even more family-bound. In politics you are liable to be overtaken at any moment by such drastic changes that both Tony and I particularly value the stability of our private life.

What can be done to improve the career position of women?

More part-time work is the obvious answer. I must admit that my initial intuitive reaction to Women's Lib was negative. But subsequently I have become aware of a drip-drip effect on my consciousness. And I am now more aware of the unfairness that is built into so many women's lives. Much as I like my women friends, I rarely have time to meet them and chat. I would think more about these things if I did. And I think I have less curiosity about wider issues than I should have.

I have always thought that part of the pleasure of being a woman is that we can have a succession of different lives. My own career has evolved without being planned.

What advice would you give to girls who want to combine family with a satisfying career?

I was never much good at preaching to others. And I tend to advance fewer views since I married a particularly analytical man. The important factor in a good marriage is to accept the other as a whole person, as he really is, as she really is. Then you can genuinely adapt to each other: combining careers with marriage is a matter of perpetual adaptation and flexibility.

I adored full-time domesticity when the children were small. It wasn't until the younger was five that I became restive, and now I'd gripe like anything if my life was confined to the purely domestic. I think most women can and should enjoy both.

Can you sum up the advantages and disadvantages of combining a family with a career in your own life?

The domestic stuff of life can provide a happy balance to the tension of outside work. But something has to give: we have let social life go. I can become exhausted and in desperate need of recharging. We've always taken separate August holidays – my husband indulging his passion for architecture, I visiting my family in America. We both need a certain amount of complete solitude.

What changes would you like to see in the future?

I am afraid I live for the present.

Denise Friedman sat behind her desk in chambers, its surface heaped with neatly rolled briefs in pink tapes. She speaks in a soft voice, but with precision and assurance. Her pale skin and dark blonde hair are set off to perfection by the black and white working clothes of a barrister.

What is most important in your life?

My family : you have to give them priority or you would end up with no family at all. My husband runs his own legal practice; my sons are eighteen and twenty-one. My career didn't become important until the younger was at school all day.

How do you manage at home?

I have always had a resident *au pair* and a daily twice a week, and I still do. I am a good organizer; I train the girls to a basic cooking routine and my daily helps to train them in housework. Several have stayed longer than a year. Although a few have got into trouble and ended up in court, I have always been on their side : we haven't had a disaster. Having a Danish Club near us has been a tremendous help : one girl has recommended another and their social life is taken care of.

Both the boys have been at day school, partly because we thought boarding school too expensive. My husband adores the children and has always enjoyed spending time with them.

What are the problems?

Although my husband is proud of me, fundamentally he believes that women should be at home : at least their work shouldn't take them out of the home more than from 11 to 3. I did not work, except on a voluntary part-time basis until the younger boy was six, partly because my husband would have felt some loss of face and partly because part-time jobs in social work, for which I had trained, were hard to come by, ridiculously so as I had lots of appropriate experience by then. That's why I turned to another profession, where I could train in hours that fitted with the family's needs instead of doing the full-time postgraduate course required in social work, regardless of your experience. The field-work requirements were impossible when the children were little, too.

We have always made a point of attending school events, I probably more so than most non-working mothers. The very few occasions when I couldn't because work had to take precedence haunt me still. And now, when one of the boys has left home early, I can't help wondering if I have always paid enough attention to them, although I thought I did at the time. Yes, I know I am tremendously conscientious and perhaps shouldn't feel guilty, but I can't help it. Decisions about whether to take a day off work or to send the ailing child to school I have always found terribly worrying. When I had embarked on my legal career my husband said, 'You have caught a tiger by the tail,' and he was right. When I was still studying part-time at Gibson's, I didn't think I would practise. Later at the pupillage stage I always left chambers at four and missed the conferences because my husband insisted I be back for the children after school, and I think he was right about that. Children are only young once. Later when I was established in chambers I never got home before six. Another problem has been criticism of friends who implied that I was neglecting my children; this made me angry but I did realize they were jealous of a woman who seemed to be using her brain. Many of them now wish that they had careers but it is too late. I don't think one could manage more than two children with a career. I don't know how people who do, cope. I do feel I am too young to be without children now and sometimes wish we had persuaded each other to have a third.

Can you say how you have achieved success in your career?

I am not at the top of my profession although I have an interesting practice and make a good income. To get to the top you have to work harder than I am prepared to do; I am not a dedicated careerist. Originally it became a matter of necessity to find a career that would fit in. I naïvely imagined that I would get school holidays free as a barrister; certainly I have more control over my time than if I had been a solicitor. It was a tremendous help to be able to discuss my studies with my husband and it was he who paid my course fees and encouraged me. It was never a problem to study alongside young students, in fact it keeps you young. Once I had started to study it was a question of desperation : I felt that if I failed one exam, I'd never pick myself up and try again. So I didn't fail one and got through quickly. I didn't get into the chambers where I did my pupillage, but the clerk liked me and scouted around. Half the battle is to get a tenancy in chambers; then the limit is up to you.

My parents were not a powerful influence, but most of the women in my family had gone to university and so I did, and I have always wanted to exercise my brain. I was never much good at school. I found my abilities late on, but in my experience if you do the work you can get through. In the last analysis I think it was my husband who propelled me. We always discussed the day's work, and I have always been interested in law.

Are there advantages in being a woman in your profession?

Without question, yes. In matrimonial work the vast majority of petitioners are women and they are prepared to tell a woman much more than a man. In criminal work women seem to go down well with juries. Women barristers seem to do best in crime and divorce. I prefer it as it does not entail much paperwork.

Are there disadvantages?

There is prejudice against women that no amount of Bills through Parliament can alter. The fact is that the Clerk in Chambers is all powerful : when a solicitor comes to him, he needn't mention your name. On the whole a solicitor has to know a woman barrister before he will ask for her because a client will choose a man unless a solicitor recommends a woman specifically. Regulations can't touch this subtle kind of discrimination. Another disadvantage is that women are undoubtedly less likely to bring business with them when they come into chambers. We are seventeen in our chambers, of which three are women. A fourth woman was opposed even by a woman because she is less likely to bring in new business.

Do women disadvantage themselves?

They are sometimes a bit slack about their appearance, which is a pity I think. Perhaps too many women give up when they marry : although this is less common than it used to be, it gave us a bad name.

To what extent are external circumstances to blame for the lack of women at the top?

The restraint of family is the main thing. Often there is paperwork to take home; sometimes you don't get briefs until 5.30 pm, and it's unsafe to make social arrangements mid-week as you may have to prepare a complicated brief the next day. Early-morning departures for trains to provincial towns are common. Conferences can drag on late. But every female appointment to a judgeship or taking silk is encouraging. Still most chambers confine themselves to the 'statutory' one; the situation is temporarily a bit better for women because of the rush to look more equal.

But husbands are the real reason. If a woman goes for the top, her husband goes. There is no end to the examples.

What can be done to improve the career prospects of women?

Work times could be made more adjustable to family commitments. Certainly there should be more part-time courses. More facilities for minding children until after five might be a good idea, but I am not happy about the farming out idea. A girl must be indoctrinated from an early age that her ability is equal to a man's.

What advice would you give to a girl who wants to combine family with a satisfying career?

Get your qualifications before you marry. I myself changed careers, for the better. But there was a connection : my sociology thesis was on juvenile delinquency.

Choose the right husband – and let him win in the end.

Can you sum up the advantages and disadvantages of combining family and career in your life?

I feel I am a fulfilled woman even after the children have gone. It is pleasant to have two incomes, in fact necessary in these days. I have paid the price of guilt; it was traumatic when my elder son went off and I still wonder if it was my fault although I don't really think so. My husband needs to put the blame somewhere. I sometimes wish we had had a third child.

What changes would you like to see in the future?

Certain administrative improvements in my profession would help women a lot. It would help if briefs could be delivered earlier, although one knows that waiting for the Crown Court lists to come out makes it difficult.

In my own career I can take a day off when I want and can take time off in the school holidays. I wish more firms would realize that women with children want to be free in school holidays and allow them to do this without pay.

When I qualified, I was able to take Part I one subject at a time. That has now changed and the Bar Council's new syllabus may make it more difficult for married women to qualify.

HUSBAND'S COMMENTS

Can you single out any special qualities possessed by your wife which have enabled her successfully to combine family life with a demanding career?

Placidity, and organizing ability to a lesser degree. If anything makes her 'flap' she keeps it a secret.

What effect, would you say, has your wife's professional involvement had on your life as a family?

She has been 'professionally' involved as a lawyer for over ten years. Before that she was 'socially' involved. So our family life has always been geared to the fact that mother has an interest in the welfare of others and to the fact that she is a person in her own right and not just a pretty face.

In the light of your own experience at home (and possibly at work) do you think it is realistic to expect an increase in the number of women who will put themselves forward to fill positions of high responsibility in the future?

Very few in my view could do this and still be able to make a male chauvinistic smoked salmon like me feel loved and needed. Many women may fill such positions as you mention and many mistresses may fill their husbands' beds as a result, if divorce doesn't intervene. I am exceptionally lucky. Sadly I think many women will prefer power to husbands.

MARY GUNTHER   PUBLIC RELATIONS DIRECTOR

Mary Gunther is a handsome, friendly woman with shoulder-length hair and a brisk but welcoming manner. When I first interviewed her she was installed in a temporary office on the site of the Hotel Inter-Continental at Hyde Park Corner festooned with cables in semi-darkness, phones ringing and workmen circulating in all directions. The traffic outside felt uncomfortably close, but nothing bothered her or diminished her enthusiasm for the subject in hand. The next time I met her, two years after our original conversation, I found her still frantically busy, but this time in a beautiful office on the first floor of the newly opened hotel.

What is most important in your life?

My daughters (who are eleven and eight), my husband, and then my career.

How do you manage at home?

I am extremely fortunate in having been married for twenty years to a very understanding man. He appreciates my personal ambitions and encourages me in every way. I think it is essential for a married career woman to have an understanding husband, someone who is prepared to help in the house, by sometimes cooking dinner, shopping, collecting the children from school and attending school events such as sports day when I am unable to do so. In our case it has been easier to arrange as my husband has his own company and therefore we can arrange our lives to fit in with our children's requirements and each other's business commitments.

We discussed the subject of children before marriage and decided to postpone having them until we had reached the situation in our careers where we could afford to cope with the extra expenditure that children entail. We were most anxious to ensure that our children should have a good home and be privately educated. We wished to be in a position to give them the best possible start in life.

I live by lists – everything is written down and planned well ahead. I also have a wonderful mother who is a devoted grandmother to the children and loves to take them out and have them to stay.

So far we have been fortunate that our plans have worked out. Our eldest daughter has passed into a leading London day school, but with the increased cost of living the battle to maintain our standards and achieve our aims becomes more and more difficult.

I would never take a job that didn't allow me to see the children off to school in the morning and we always have nursery tea together when I get back. At this time we talk about their day and I check on the homework, projects and their social lives. They have their own nursery diary so parties, expeditions and visits to the dentist, etc. are all on record.

What are the problems?

My husband's requirements sometimes conflict with the children's and I have to balance them – sometimes my husband comes first, such as a holiday in the sun on our own, and at other times the children, though obviously I try to spend as much time with them as I can. Much as I loved them as babies, I find that they are more interesting to me as they grow older and develop as individuals. I like helping them with homework and taking them to museums and enjoying new experiences with them – I do miss them terribly when they go away on holidays, and I try to arrange for my own time off to coincide with theirs, but this is not always possible.

Can you say how you have achieved success in your career?

Hard work, perseverance, self-discipline. I have benefited from the fact that public relations is a good field for a woman; equal pay and equal opportunity up to a point. Few women until now have made Board level, but I hope I will. There is no point in working if there is no goal in sight.

I was, I suppose, one of the first girls of my generation to have a career as well as being married with children. Uppermost in our minds has always been the deep conviction that our children should have a stable home, and the same educational opportunities that we had. I feel very strongly that there is nothing better that I can do for my children than educate them to be self-sufficient, well-adjusted and happy people.

I had the good fortune to have exceptionally far-sighted parents, and was given an excellent education equal to that of my brothers. My home life was also extremely happy, and this start to my life has given me the necessary strength and willpower to succeed, and with the educational qualifications, the tools with which to work.

I had the financial incentive especially in the early stages of my marriage and career, of wanting a high standard of living, buying a house, good help and so on. We had to work for that and we work as equal partners.

Are there advantages in being a woman in your profession?

Very much so. Women are often better at making friends and communicating than men. They are used to getting on with all kinds of people – shopkeepers, the dustmen and so on. Women are creative, often good at writing, good tempered and have organizing abilities – all important assets in this area. Public Relations is a particularly good field for women because in many ways it is an extension of one's personal life – good manners and thoughtfulness are most important.

Any disadvantages in being a woman in your career?

It is difficult for married women to go on courses at weekends and attend functions without their husbands in the evenings – this might hinder promotion. Usually we can only get to the bottom of the top. It is very frustrating to know the right answers and not be able to implement them. I enjoy decision making, but big policy decisions are too often regarded as a male preserve. I moved to my present job at the Hotel Inter-Continental London because

I am totally involved with the whole project and can make decisions that count. I like to take responsibility and carry the rap as well as getting the credit.

Do women disadvantage themselves?

Unfortunately some do. I feel denigrated myself (and I think many other career women do) when some females over-emphasize sex. I can't stand the 'false eyelash' approach in the office, although it is important to look attractive. I also think playing on health is out of place. If one has health problems, see a doctor. It must not become a handicap, a bore to one's employer and one's colleagues.

To what extent are outside circumstances to blame for the lack of women at the top?

Parents set your goals. Unenlightened or unintelligent parents make a terrible difference. Girls are often badly advised at school, by so-called careers teachers, though this seems to be slowly improving as women gain recognition in various fields. Most of my friends don't work . . . some men are terrified of independent women. Some men disapprove of me!

What can be done to improve the career position of women?

As more women are seen to be successful, more will try to succeed. Equal opportunities and education are the only ways to bring about this essential change so it will be a slow progress. My brothers never made their own beds, but nowadays more boys are trained to help in the house. We are supposed now to be equal in sex but there is a long way to go for real equality. Specifically I would like to see certain changes: maternity leave by right; tax allowances for domestic help; large companies should have more playgroups and crèches to give those women without home help time to continue their careers. The re-grading of staff to avoid paying women equally is already in hand in many organizations – this should be stopped. Blind prejudice must go – why shouldn't women work in unusual jobs if they have the qualifications, why shouldn't a woman drive a bus if she wants to?

What is your personal advice to girls who want to have children and a satisfying career?

Postpone having babies. Don't worry about fertility or pleasing your in-laws. I waited nearly ten years. Get established and get plenty of working experience. It is much more difficult to start a worthwhile career later, even at thirty. Many of my friends who had their families early and whose children are now grown up and away from home are bored stiff, and often lonely – some are trying to start a career but it is not easy. Statistically also, most women will be widowed and those not used to coping with life find the going extremely hard – both financially and practically.

What would you like to see in the future?

I believe that the more successful women there are the better. I'd like to see Margaret Thatcher and Shirley Williams as Prime Ministers – and more women in politics, although the many late-night sittings in Parliament make it difficult if one is married with young children.

What advantages have you found in having both career and family?

A higher standard of living for the family and job satisfaction. Wives who do have this don't go looking for lovers and adventures : a career can make a marriage more stable !

Any disadvantages?

I have had health problems, which I attribute to overwork. One must be wife, mother, mistress, career woman, hostess, cook, gardener and general help. Also three miscarriages – but who is to say work was to blame? With both my daughters I worked until one week before their births, and the day my first daughter was born I sat up in bed surrounded by printers preparing a Christmas catalogue for Liberty's, the Regent Street store. When I joined Harrods as Head of Public Relations I was six months pregnant, and the management were extremely kind to me even if the customers were a little surprised ! In both cases I took two months off work to recover and then returned to my desk leaving nanny in charge! School holidays are always a problem, and I would like to spend more time with the children then.

Have you any final comments?

I have been happily married to the same man for twenty years. My family is the most important thing in my life. I cannot say that too often. But also I am my own person. My parents made sure of that.

HUSBAND'S COMMENTS

Can you single out any special qualities possessed by your wife which have enabled her to successfully combine family life with a demanding career?

Capacity to organize.

What effect, would you say, has your wife's professional involvement had on your life as a family?

We have always agreed mutually on any important factor in our lives, and for this reason we have never allowed either of our careers to come before our family life.

In the light of your own experience at home (and possibly at work) do you think it is realistic to expect an increase in the number of women who will put themselves forward to fill positions of high responsibility in the future?

Yes.

In spite of a busy morning, culminating in a Working Party on Truancy, Anne Jones talked enthusiastically over a salad lunch (produced by her secretary) in her office, which is as bright and friendly as she is. She had 600 reports waiting to be written, and a session with a neighbouring junior head on playgrounds to fit in, but she concentrated on our conversation with an easy warmth and freshness. Anne Jones is joint author of Male and Female : Choosing your Role in Modern Society, *and* Living Choices, *two CRAC publications.*

What is most important in your life?

My family : by that I mean my husband and children. They help me feel secure and real. To me relationships with people I love and who love me are vital to a satisfying life. I work because that makes me feel useful and fulfilled.

How do you manage at home with three children and a husband?

I have learnt to delegate the labour of running the home so that I can concentrate my energy on relationships with the members of the family. The children are now thirteen, twelve and nine. I didn't work full-time till after the youngest was at school all day; even then I chose a job near her school so that I took her to school and fetched her till she was eight years old. One of the reasons why I decided to be a teacher originally was because I knew it would fit in with having a family. Our children are secure enough to cope with having a mother like me : in relationships like this I've always felt it's quality not quantity that counts.

We've had an *au pair* girl for the last nine years. I've learnt to make her job important and satisfying to her. So many *au pairs* are given just the grotty boring jobs and no real opportunity for exercising initiative, decision-making and taking responsibility. Our girl finds her work satisfying because it is important and we value it. On the other hand, I take care not to overwork her and I always reward her if there are extras like helping with a party, or looking after a child with a minor illness. It takes about two months to train a new girl each year, including teaching her to do simple cooking – and then allowing her to experiment with exotic recipes if she is keen. I usually show her how I do things and itemize the jobs to be done, she then works out her own methods, but knows what the end result should be. It's always a strain at first but worth it : by the end of the year, the girls have usually matured and developed enormously. We have all the electric gadgets possible to make the housework as light as possible. I delegate to the *au pair* the routine tasks – tidying, vacuuming, washing, ironing and some cooking – without any compunction. I tried putting on a family supper at 7 pm but that was too late for the children to fit in all their homework and hobbies. So they have a high tea at 5 pm, usually watching children's TV at the same time, and then are rested and ready to chatter with me or play. They are secure in this routine, knowing I will arrive between 4.30 and 6 pm and will have time for them when they've finished eating. They do prefer me to be there even if they're busy doing their own thing.

I love cooking : my husband and I usually eat quite late; we don't have to wash up as we have a dishwasher. I have become more efficient about cooking : I usually cook three times the quantity that we need and put two meals away for a busy day or a sudden spontaneous supper party; my husband can invite a business colleague home for supper knowing that we won't be stuck for food and that it won't exhaust me either. On Sunday we always have a ritual traditional roast and pudding; sometimes we entertain friends as well. The children often help then because they enjoy cooking : if a lot of people are coming, they like to help set the table. We don't do this to exploit them, but to give a good feeling of being a family working together.

My husband has recently started doing the weekly shopping on a Saturday morning. He began when I was ill once but found he enjoys it – buying in bulk, juggling with best buys. He's much more patient and careful about it than I am. It's a tremendous help. It has taken me a long time to allow my husband, children and *au pair* to help as much as they now do : the idea that it was my job and my duty to look after my husband and children totally myself was very ingrained in me. I didn't expect or ask anyone to help for ages : very stupid of me ! I still get pleasure from looking after the others though and feel deprived if I can't ! Cooking satisfies my homemaking instincts, and gardening satisfies my need for peace, creativity and exercise.

What are the problems?

Learning to delegate without feeling guilty or deprived. Giving enough attention and care to each member of the family. Our youngest sometimes feels she doesn't quite see enough of me. I'm not sure she sees any more of me when I am at home in the holidays without any help because then the chores take over ! I'm certainly very much more tired now I am a headmistress than I was when I had a less onerous job. I try to get home for tea if we have an evening meeting at school. I try to have a bedtime chat with each of the children. Sometimes it is a nuisance having to do paperwork for school later in the evening, but fortunately my husband also brings work home sometimes. When he is away on business I work extra hard so that I am free to be with him when he is there.

Can you say how you have achieved success in your career?

I couldn't have done it without my husband's support. He persuaded me to apply for this headship – I was not sure whether I would cope ! His confidence in me is very strengthening. My mother has always encouraged me too : she's a wonderful, versatile person, who also worked when we were young. She made me realize the importance of *not* sticking at a level below one's ability, the ridiculousness of hiding one's capability. It isn't success so much as self-actualization which motivates me. It's obvious to me that many women in previous generations sacrificed themselves for the sake of the children – but it often wasn't worth it.

I must say that I think my greatest period of development began when I stopped teaching and stayed at home to look after the children. Curiously enough many of the skills I find most useful now were developed at this time : flexibility, stamina, tolerance, versatility. During this period I took up further studies in sociology, became a marriage-guidance counsellor and was very active in local community affairs, particularly in Advancement of State Education (CASE) and in voluntary work. Combining all this with being a mother, housewife, part-time school counsellor, gardener, decorator, author, friend and local Ombudswoman, was excellent training for being a headmistress! I had to be well-organized yet utterly flexible, capable of switching from the serious to the ridiculous and back in no time. I began to learn how to use that part of myself appropriate to the task in hand, to keep calm, and keep things in perspective. I learnt to cope with stress, uncertainty and being imperfect; essential qualities if you are to hold down a big job, where you are constantly under pressure. I wasn't consciously training myself, of course. But many housewives *undervalue* what they have learnt from being at home and from being mature and experienced : it is of inestimable value.

It's fortunate that my husband is highly successful in his job : that is important to me, for I feel I don't constitute a threat to him, and therefore I don't have to hold back for fear of putting him down. We share some similar managerial problems and often help each other by listening, and understanding what the other is saying.

Are there advantages in being a woman in the teaching profession?

Teaching fits in with family hours. It doesn't end at 4 pm of course, but there is flexibility after that. Basically I keep the same hours as the children. We even do our homework together sometimes.

I do think being married and a mother helps a woman to keep a sense of proportion. It also helps me keep in touch with my feelings. It is a pity that so many women are afraid to apply for top jobs for fear of what it will do to them : fear of being the 'stereotyped' headmistress, fear of being cut off from friends. I haven't found this to be the case, though I shared these fears before I took up my post. In fact I find I need to see my friends more than ever. So often women devalue their experience at home, and in the community, or are conditioned to think of themselves always in a supportive role, as second-class citizens. It's a pity.

Are there disadvantages?

Sometimes it is difficult for married women to go on training courses, or stay late : that could be a disadvantage professionally; but this is more of a myth than a fact in this day and age. Men are far more helpful at home and tolerant than they used to be.

Do women disadvantage themselves?

Sometimes women equate success with loss of femininity : this is nonsense. Yet women often put themselves down, try not to compete with men, feel guilty : this kind of behaviour will undermine professional competence unnecessarily. Women in conflict dither and give out ambivalent signals, which is confusing. Conflicts will exist, of course, but they can be minimized if you work at them. It is often a question of motivation : when a woman says she can't stay late for a meeting, it probably means she doesn't really want to. Women should abandon the 'I must do everything' approach at home and delegate more. They should expect more co-operation and partnership from their husband and children. Women who leave all the decision-making to men are unnecessarily bad at making up their minds; some women fuss too much, pay too much attention to detail : I don't think men flap so much. But it all boils down to women's confidence in themselves. What we have to develop is the courage to take risks for ourselves. Then we learn.

To what extent are external factors to blame for the lack of women at the top?

Social conditioning from early childhood makes women hold back. I am appalled by the low aspirations among the adolescent girls at my school. When a woman applies for a senior post, it is still difficult to convince employers that she is a safe bet and not a risk. I must say that the Inner London Education Authority

D

(which appointed me) has shown a great deal of courage and vision in the appointments it has made recently : women do really seem to have a chance; so do young men.

What can be done to improve the career position of women?

The short answer is to change people's attitudes. Most people think that being an administrator is a dull job to do with shuffling paper : it's not. It is to do with people and requires considerable interpersonal skills at which women often excel.

I am particularly interested too in the conditioning processes which govern our attitudes to sex roles : that's why I have helped with a work-book for adolescents on this topic. The book will help a little, but the effects will probably be marginal, for to look at causes is not to remove them.

Have you advice to offer to girls who want to have both children and a satisfying career?

The biggest con of all is to give up everything for others. Be true to yourself. Look at examples of women who have achieved and see how they manage, get help if you can, and delegate all you can. I happen to think it is important to be at home with the children when they are young : but many mums who spend all their time at home see little of their children because they get so absorbed in the chores, or bored and dispirited. It is very important to do something outside the home, whatever it may be : it helps you to keep in touch with reality. Any enjoyable experience is valuable later. We need to take in if we are going to continue to give out.

Can you sum up some of the advantages and disadvantages of combining family and career in your life?

Being a mother and running a complex household was an important part of my training for my present job. So work is a natural extension of my family life. My husband, who is very successful and has a very demanding job himself, enjoys my success. He has helped to show me I must make my own decisions and supports me in them. We discuss our work problems on an equal footing with great mutual respect. I am much less tense than I was as Deputy, when I felt I was under-functioning.

I like being well-paid even though so much of my income goes on domestic help, tax, and more extravagant buying because of pressures of time. I would hate to do a job that didn't fulfil me – I would rather not work at all.

What changes would you like to see in the future?

It is ridiculous that working women do not get a tax allowance for home help. There should be a recognized training leading to professional status and proper rates of pay for workers who would provide housekeeping and child care services in the home. I believe there are a lot of women around, young and older (perhaps with grown-up children), who would really enjoy this kind of work, possibly on a day-visiting basis. I think it is important to look after one's own children, but when a woman starts to go back to work she needs as much help as she can get if she is not to get over-tired.

I hope the book I have helped write about male and female roles will help change fundamental attitudes. At the very least young people should have the opportunity to look at the conditioning processes that assign sex roles and then accept or reject them. Shared responsibility in the home is more common than it used to be. I think men haven't been allowed to be as caring or as helpful as they might be. Women have monopolized the caring roles but this can and is being modified.

ELIZABETH NELSON   Market Research Director

Elizabeth Nelson runs her own market research company, Taylor Nelson Associates. She is highly qualified, having taken a BA in Psychology and a Ph.D. in Clinical Psychology in the USA and in England respectively, and her male colleagues speak of her professional achievements with awe. To her friends she is a most relaxed, informal and lively person, with an infectious laugh and a great gift for creating an atmosphere of fun and putting people at their ease. We talked in her glass-fronted study in the far corner of her open-plan, first-floor living-room, while her children were sitting round the dining-table at the other end, doing their homework, supervised by her schoolteacher husband.

Can you say what is most important in your life?

Trying to be a well-rounded person. I really think I am more concerned now than I was before in running a happy home : I'm more interested in being able to cook, knowing something about cricket and football to keep up with the boys – as well as running my business. I think there has been a shift in my position – quite unconsciously – and that the entrepreneurial impetus has died somewhat, giving way to other things. The age of the children partly accounts for this – they're more interesting now and I participate more in their lives.

How do you manage your home now and how did you manage in the past?

In the past I had a nanny-housekeeper who did everything – literally ran the house. If it hadn't been for her I couldn't have got through my work. Since my divorce [and remarriage] the situation has changed : I now have to manage with an *au pair* which means doing all the chores at weekends, stocking up at the cash-and-carry and cooking for the deep-freeze (she does the daily shopping but that doesn't amount to much). Having an *au pair* is really like having another child who needs your constant attention. This creates problems : it makes it more difficult to do justice to other relationships, for instance with the children. I also think they have become more demanding – or I am more conscious of it now. When I am at home they want *my* attention and they make this quite obvious.

What are the special problems of combining a full-time job with running a family?

Finding time to do all the things that have to be done, especially the 'little' things like buying the odd spare parts for my sons' bicycles or radios or playing football with them. Fortunately my husband, who is a teacher, helps a lot and he takes over a lot of the homework supervision. Having an open-plan house is a disadvantage in a way as there never seem to be enough 'private' places. In other ways it helps : it creates a working atmosphere at night when the children all sit round the dining-table, working.

Can you say how you achieved success in your career?

Sheer slogging; very, very hard work. I worked harder than anyone else around. My doctorate probably helped – it was a good springboard and got me into Mars which was wonderful training. After Mars I spent another nine years in an advertising agency, then towards the end of that time I decided to set up on my own. I think one of the reasons was that my father had his own business – a small, highly efficient, highly profitable one. This was very important to me and a great influence. The final decision was almost made for me : when I announced that I was pregnant the firm immediately brought in a managing director to take my place (I had been managing director of one of their subsidiary companies). They never envisaged that I might want to carry on, which I found both unfair and unimaginative. When I left I took the best people with me – you might call it ruthless or underhanded, the sort of thing 'a man would do'. There was some talk that I would be sued for enticement of staff, but this never came to anything. After starting my own firm I found I was pregnant again, with number three! That really threw me.

Are there advantages in being a woman in your profession?

Certainly. Part of my job is to understand why housewives do what they do. Market research is a new profession and we are forever making progress in getting new uses of survey techniques. I am thinking here of people in the City, like insurance companies and merchant banks, who are just beginning to use surveys among the general public. Very often a woman in a new field can bring a new approach and has an advantage in this respect.

Are there disadvantages?

Yes, pregnancy. You can't go to see a client when you are eight months pregnant. Then there are times when I'm making a presentation and am aware that a woman hasn't been into that dining-room before. This makes me behave less like a woman, or what I think would be less like a woman seen through men's eyes. A severe disadvantage, also, is that there is no career structure in market research. What happens is that very brilliant male market researchers can easily move into 'marketing', leaving women in market research. There is a shortage of good people and this means that a woman who has had some experience can get back into market research, but she is limited in terms of status and salary compared to her former male colleagues who have gone into marketing in a large company.

Do you think women disadvantage themselves?

Some women are quite terrifyingly aggressive. There are a lot of women high up in market research and some of them get a kick out of cutting colleagues down to size.

To what extent do you think outside circumstances are to blame for the lack of women at the top?

If we mean quotas in medical schools, etc. – yes, of course. This is partly women's own fault. A lot of them don't have the desire or the motivation. This is a pity as they have an enormous contribution to make.

What can be done to improve the career position of women?

More training and retraining later in life, and better quality career advice. I would like to see more women given a chance to train as social workers to cope with the increasingly complicated problems in our society. I think that women over the age of thirty-five are uniquely placed to do this.

What would be your personal advice to girls who want to have children and a satisfying career?

That I must look at in terms of my own daughter. Don't marry too young; try and get the highest qualification you possibly can, including vocational qualifications; gain some experience and at least have a foot on the career ladder before having your children.

What changes would you like to see in the future?

I would like to see the greater symmetry now found in the home carried over into jobs and careers. I should like to see a greater sharing of tasks, increasing awareness that men and women work as members of a team. Women should not be seen as being identical to men but should be valued for themselves, for their special contribution. I believe that in every job women have a special contribution they can make, as catalysts, interpreters, etc. I don't want to see differences made to disappear – these differences make for enrichment.

What advantages have you personally found in having both a career and a family?

That's where I came in. I want to be well-rounded and I think having a career as well as a family has helped me with that – it has given me perspective which I feel privileged to have. Also, I think I understand my husband better as a result of working with male colleagues.

Any disadvantages?

Yes. Increasingly I feel torn between the needs of the children and the job. But probably in ten years' time this will no longer be so.

HUSBAND'S COMMENTS

Can you single out any special qualities possessed by your wife which have enabled her to successfully combine family life with a demanding career?

The making of lists and sometimes even the making of lists of lists! She is so methodical and plans with such furious determination that there is little chance of anything preventing her business efficiency from carrying over to the smooth running of domestic affairs and family life.

However when something does go awry, such as keys being mislaid or even a brief-case, then this is such a contrast to the otherwise machine-like precision of life, that hysteria can rapidly set in. But life is never dull!

What effect, would you say, has your wife's professional involvement had on your life as a family?

There are times when the rest of the family recognize that Liz is working under pressure and make special efforts to lower the tension. These can be positive, such as having a drink ready or the table laid when she gets home, or negative like just keeping out of the way. There is a spirit of closeness and co-operation at such times.

It also has a tremendous influence on the range and variety of social contacts and on the self-assurance of the children when meeting strangers. They have also had the opportunity to enjoy extensive travel when school holidays have coincided with conferences, etc.

In the light of your own experience at home (and possibly at work) do you think it is realistic to expect an increase in the number of women who will put themselves forward to fill positions of high responsibility in the future?

I think there will be a slow and gradual increase in the numbers of women in positions of high responsibility, but I think there is still a very large reservoir of opinion, even among those younger women who are at work full-time, that marriage and home and family are their first priorities. Even among older women at work and especially among those who have returned to work after raising a family, there is a reluctance to apply for positions of responsibility and, I think, a prejudice against appointing them.

Marjorie Proops was at home in her exquisite and cosy house, very private, with a lovely garden for sitting out in to match. She is handsome and elegant as befits a one-time fashion artist, but her affability is the most striking thing about her. She tilts her cigarette holder at a humorous angle; everything about her is disarming. At the same time she misses nothing, which renders her pervasive magnanimity the more refreshing. Her husband was there too and couldn't resist chipping in, which added to the fun.

Can you say what is most important in your life?

All through my life, if there has been a dilemma or hard decision to make, I have chosen family. But I have always had a compelling need to work outside the home.

How did you manage at home when your son was growing up – and now?

When he was born I was luckily freelancing and didn't have to go out to work. My husband installed us in farmhouse digs not far from my parents at Windsor before he went off to war. I had an arrangement with an elderly lady in Windsor who I met off the 7.30 am bus on the days I had to go to London. I'd cycle off to Slough Station knowing that she would stay on if anything happened – those were hazardous days – and the farm family was always ready to back me up if needed. But if she couldn't come I stayed at home.

The fashion drawings were a slog, mostly on commission, and I often worked far into the night. I found I could work best when Robert was safely in bed. My husband thought he had chosen a safe place for us, but we received no less than twenty-two incendiaries while we were there and the roof came in one night. Social life was negligible, but Wednesday afternoons were a high spot when we went off to the matinee at Windsor and had cups of tea at the theatre. As soon as the bombs stopped I returned to London and became a salaried journalist with the encouragement of the editor of the *Daily Herald*.

At this point I found a living-in mother's help who stayed with us for years. It is essential to have a relationship with a paid helper – you must convince them that the surrogate role is invaluable and that they are involved with the family. It is a natural instinct with me; I get involved with people anyway and did not have to set out to achieve this deliberately. Latterly I've tried various sorts like *au pairs* but I find that I become their surrogate mother – so I hope for older ladies nowadays.

As far as housework is concerned, I would always have paid anyone to do it. I do it at the weekends and quite like it when I don't have to do it, but the housework must be done. There are two sorts of women and I am the kind that cannot do with squalor.

What are the problems?

To this day I seek reassurance from my son – I have suffered from the guilt inseparable from working mothers.

The cucumber-sandwich syndrome is the family joke. When Robert was about six he asked me why I wasn't like other mothers making cucumber sandwiches for tea. I had a frightful night, nudging Proops awake, but he said it was a decision for me. But we agreed that I would end up irritable and impatient and maybe resentful if I gave up work. I tried to explain to Robert that anyone can make cucumber sandwiches and from the beginning he knew where I worked – he was spoiled by my colleagues and loved coming to the office or ringing me up. It is important that your children should know the kind of life you are leading when you are not with them and then the mystery and threat disappear. Of course, newspaper offices are fun anyway.

Then there was the problem, not particularly affected by my career, of the father returning after all those years away; it was an uneasy relationship for a time, some hostility and jealousy was unavoidable with such a dramatic change; the classic post-war situation. But I do think one tends to compensate doubly a child because one is going out to work, and so in Robert's case there was a danger of his feeling doubly rejected.

We sent our son to boarding school when he was thirteen, which I think we would have done anyway as he is an only child. We had tried boarding school earlier, but briefly as it was not a success. We chose one not too far away that allowed week-end passes and we saw more of him than most parents. He became self-reliant and made friends. I think children are fine if they grow to understand that what you are doing is not in conflict with their interests and always provided the family relationships are stable. They must know they can rely on you when they need you.

Can you say how you have achieved success in your career?

Partly luck, and choosing the right husband – that is luck too. A well-adjusted grown-up man who is tolerant and fair-minded has everything to do with his wife's success. My husband is a man before his time, prepared to share in everything and totally practical. Sharing comes naturally to him, not as a gesture, not as a favour; I feel sorry for the women whose husbands wave tea-towels occasionally.

My approach to my work has been important; I am dedicated and prepared to work all night if I have to, and I still often do. I have never minded what sort of job I have done, I would never ask anyone else to do what I wouldn't do myself (except type, a skill I regrettably lack), and I have never had an inflated idea of my own importance. I have been lucky to have had plenty of energy, but I have also always worked hard. I have always been lucky in the people I have worked with; as I describe in my book *Dear Marje* I have been helped and encouraged at every turn, ever since the war when my career was pretty stagnant. Success may have to do with my liking passionately what I do.

I have tried to be a campaigning journalist and have always been a political activist. I was sometimes the only woman attending union meetings – that was at the time before I gained hiring and firing powers that I have now. I am proud to have helped get widows' pensions raised and promoted law reforms like the Homosexual Law, Divorce Law, and equal pay for women. I am proud of working with the Finer Committee on one-parent families. Journalists have a platform and can be influential but I have some regrets about not entering political life. Parliamentary office hours are all wrong for women with families.

Are there advantages to being a woman in your profession?

Apart from a certain rarity value, no. On the contrary, women are enormously patronized. But the fact that women are on the whole not as tough as men is an advantage to everyone in some ways. It fascinates me how men will sharpen their wits on a news story regardless: no holds barred if it has news value. Whereas women will show more compassion. I cannot bear unsavoury digging into people's lives and often feel it is intrusion. My men colleagues think I am soft.

Are there disadvantages?

The biggest is that men don't take women as seriously as they should. It has taken editors – who are invariably men – years to decide that women can write on serious subjects. Until recently they were under the impression that women's interests were restricted to trivial subjects – not to mention forgetting that men have a trivial side too, thank God; how dull and colourless we should all be otherwise – think of the Chinese! If I have achieved anything at all in journalism it is in convincing the men for whom I have worked that women can be serious, can be objective and analytical.

In a male-oriented profession I have had to plead and connive in order to be listened to, to overcome the conditioning and prejudices; everybody's unconscious assumption that it is men who take the decisions. Even now, when I am an executive of my paper, I feel I am always the statutory woman. It is still a struggle to exert influence. To give a minor example, I could not persuade my editor to abandon the campaign someone dreamed up to revive the mini skirt; if it had been for women's own good I would have been all for it, but this was exploitation in my opinion – something to leer at. I keep hoping men will grow out of this sort of attitude but it is an uphill struggle.

Do women disadvantage themselves?

Oh yes. They fall into traps. Realizing they have a battle on their hands, as indeed they have, they take up weapons to get their own way. They are unable to be true to themselves – it is false role playing – and so they can become unattractive as people. This easily happens to anyone who achieves power, but I fear that women are even more likely to lose their heads in this way because they are unaccustomed to it, and get carried away. Women journalists have a tough and boozy image – but only a few are like this. Most of us go home in the evenings and enjoy domestic life.

To what extent are external circumstances to blame for the lack of women at the top?

There is no doubt that the majority of men want women to stay where they are. Most men feel threatened and will go on fighting to prevent women from achieving a pre-eminent position. Girls are disadvantaged in their education, reflecting the prevailing male view, but that is improving. And, of course, there are the practical problems inherent in raising a family, not to be under-estimated.

What can be done to improve the career position of women?

I wish I had the answers. I think it is going to be a long slow battle: I see it as a war of attrition, a war of nerves. We must drip away at men. Women of influence must encourage and support the younger ones coming along. It has taken five years for the Equal Pay Act to become law. The Equal Opportunities Act could make it even harder for women – clever employers are already taking avoiding action, there are plenty of loopholes. But what will improve is women's attitude towards themselves.

Of course there is a danger of women losing their feminine power over men in the battle for supremacy. I know a psychiatrist who is concerned about the side effect of the damage to relationships with men. He tells me that some women are making demands on men, including sexual demands, that men cannot meet. Women may learn to become less dependent on men for everything. It seems that if we take two steps forward we must always take one back.

What advice would you give to girls who want to have children and a satisfying career?

A lot do write and ask me and I tell them they must be prepared to make sacrifices. In the first place I remind them that father is an indispensable part of the plan : marry or live with a man who wants for you what you want for yourself. You must be prepared to be totally dedicated to both parts of your life, work and family. In fact you have to be two people rolled into one. Have you noticed that successful people of both sexes are at least two people? (I have always wanted to be domestic at weekends. You have to be careful that the homemaking part of your life never disappears.) And remember that most men, like my husband and my son, like an ordered life. If you provide them with this you provide yourself with the powerful feeling of an ongoing family relationship which doesn't change when the young leave home. I cheerfully helped my son to pack when he decided it was time to live away from home and he has never stopped wanting to return home when there is the opportunity.

Can you sum up the pros and cons of combining family and career in your life?

Not everyone can manage to be two people rolled into one. When I look around I see very few women in my profession who have husbands and children as well. As for politicians – I can hardly think of one! You have to be good at switching on and off. You have to learn to conserve your energy. When I see a grey face in the mirror I tell myself to get undressed and go to bed; it is essential to avoid exhaustion. One gives up some social life – especially as one gets older and I do miss it; but I have found I can't cope otherwise. One hangs on to one's friends who understand and don't expect me to cook them dinner every time. I find

I need the therapy of needlework and embroidery and I value the little walks I take with the dog. But it is a necessity for me to work and I still take only one day off. My husband understands me and supports me utterly.

What changes would you like to see in the future?

I want my grandchildren to grow up in a world without want or misery: I want Utopia. But to be going on with, the young can be better conditioned to accept equality of the sexes, by their parents and by their education. My grandson and granddaughter attend the same school, which I am glad of. I disapprove of single-sex schools although my son was happy at one. I can already discern that my granddaughter is going to be all right; at six she is determined. I dislike unhealthy competition between people – surely we can replace it with something better? And I loathe poverty and would love to end the despair of old age. I would love not to be the recipient of nearly 50,000 problems a year!

HUSBAND'S COMMENTS

Can you single out any special qualities possessed by your wife which have enabled her to successfully combine family life with a demanding career?

A capacity for hard work, ability to cope with complicated and sometimes conflicting demands on her thoughts and time and an empathy which secures the co-operation of her associates both in the office and at home.

What effect, would you say, has your wife's professional involvement had on your life as a family?

Widened our horizons both in professional and social contacts and in material terms has given a greater sense of security.

In the light of your own experience at home (and possibly at work) do you think it is realistic to expect an increase in the number of women who will put themselves forward to fill positions of high responsibility in the future?

No. Biological and social patterns, the former of which cannot be changed, severely limit the number of individuals who can or will have the capacity to put themselves forward for positions of high responsibility.

Ursula Sedgwick, Senior Associate Director in a major advertising agency, is chatty and approachable, radiating good sense. She has a briskness about her that falls short of bossiness, but her air of authority is tempered by a jolly smile and casual clothes that suit her beautifully. She relaxed in an armchair while the Siamese cats and the Jack Russell strolled about.

Can you say what is most important in your life?

My family. I see all four of them together (husband, a managing director, and three sons, twenty-three, twenty and nineteen). If it came to a crunch – which it hasn't – the job would go completely. On a day-to-day basis my job is terribly important to me. I feel I must do it well and give my employers value for money. I did give up a job which I loved, years ago, because I realized it wouldn't fit in with having children, and besides my husband and I practically never met. I was one of the very small number of six women who were on news in Fleet Street at the time. Anne Scott-James arrived at the *Express* a bit later : she made a tremendous difference, establishing the woman's position. In those days we despised the magazines and the woman's page was only just allowable. To give you an idea, after I was married my News Editor wanted to send me to Manchester : when I demurred he asked me which I put first, my job or my home? When I returned the question to him, he was furious! (I expect he felt guilty.)

How do you manage at home?

My husband and I have always shared the domestic chores on Saturday mornings and enjoy it thoroughly. I think he has done everything except laundry and I have done everything except the

car. I hate doing anything alone. When we had a nanny she
would always have Saturday afternoon and Sundays off and this
always worked extremely well until we tried housekeepers as the
boys grew up : they were disastrous so we reverted to mother's
helps. I am still in touch with nearly all of them.

I have battled for maternity leaves for years : I had partly won
by the time our second was born. My husband collected me after
work as usual at six and he was born at home at a quarter to
nine. Before the first I had to resign and was only taken back
three months later on condition that I employed a permanent
living-in nanny, which was very sensible of my boss. I interviewed
at least thirty women, looking for the cosy old thing that I had
had, and who ran my mother's family for fifty-four years. But I
quickly learned that you should employ someone who is younger
than yourself, whom you like regardless of her qualifications and
who preferably is British.

What are the problems?

I remember a most exhausting period when the three children
were under four and a half. I gave up my lunch hour for a year
in order to collect the eldest from nursery school and deliver him
back to the nanny. I remember a dismal period when we employed housekeepers when the boys were at day prep school : the
housekeepers put the care of the house way ahead of care of the
children. Then when they were all at boarding school the home
helps didn't like being alone most of the time and after consulting
with the boys we decided to do without, except for cleaning help.

I once made the mistake of employing a German nanny which
held up the infant's development for a time because she expected
obedience above all things and didn't know nursery rhymes and
so on.

Some people were determined to make me feel guilty even
though I knew I should have been bored stiff on my own at
home : my brain becomes dulled in no time if I haven't got other
wits to sharpen them on. If a baby cried when I came home the
nanny was inclined to say, 'He's been so good all day' : infuriat-
ing. You do feel almost physically deprived, leaving the baby
when you first go back to work, like being without a lover

perhaps; but you quickly grow accustomed to the separation. I managed to choose good nannies but I shall never forget some of the awful women I interviewed : they nearly all wanted to see the pram, very few wanted to see the baby.

Can you say how you have achieved success in your career?

Hard work and a determination not to give up. I have always had a real horror of not being independent. I recall a friend married to a rich man who couldn't even buy a dress, never mind the piano she longed for. And it may be reaction to my mother and her friends : that generation seemed to me to have been brought up incapable of doing anything; it seems to have been the fashion, whereas my grandmother knew how to do everything she asked her servants to do. My mother couldn't even wash her own hair. My grandmother, who influenced my upbringing tremendously, was maddening but immensely capable and had done things like helping in the early days in Czechoslovakia. She would have been a Women's Libber. My father too was keen that each of his children should be well equipped with education and encouraged me to go to university. When I wanted to start a family I consulted my friends about leaving and getting back later and they all advised me it was hopeless : you lose ground all the time or you slip into a backwater. I was not going to settle for something second-best and I knew I had the capacity. I am still irritated by the many women who settle for rank below their capability : for one thing it is not fair on the employer who needs all the top skill he can get and for another it lets the side of womankind down. Some of these half-hearted middle-rank people refuse promotion on the grounds of their family life but I know you can give both 100 per cent and I regard this as an excuse. Who can say that because you give less than your best to one aspect of your life, you are giving of your best in another? I think the reverse is apt to be the case.

I have enjoyed all of it even though I am falling into the 'token senior woman' period and have had to settle for something short of the top. My successors will be able to overtake me because the climate is changing so rapidly. My success must be attributed also to economic need : that was the spur in the beginning but once you have started on that trail you can't get off : your living standard rises to match your earnings. It is possible that the attitudes to women I experienced in earlier years – I have been working in the firm for twenty-five years – may have made me work harder. And I used to meet the reaction that if you worked you couldn't be a good mother. I ignored this mostly but it did make me determined to prove them wrong. For instance I always baked magnificent goodies for my children's birthday parties.

Are there advantages in being a woman in your profession?

Yes, especially in earlier times when it was special to be a 'normal' married woman and there was some mystique ridiculously still attached to cooking and other womanly pursuits which was considered useful to colleagues as we were all trying to sell products to housewives. Nowadays the sexes have more shared experiences. But I still think that women have far more in common with each other than men do and so communication is freer among us; so being a woman could be said to be a considerable advantage in my profession where the clientele is largely made up of women after all.

Are there disadvantages?

Male colleagues are happier to see women as seconds, whatever they may be doing. They may protest but it is true. When I complained to a colleague about not being on the Board, he was surprised : 'You've done very well for a woman,' he said.

Do women disadvantage themselves?

Too often they are not prepared to take the job seriously enough; I think it is cheating not to give of your best. Too many won't put themselves forward for promotion. Of course the younger ones frequently undervalue themselves. For a few it is not worth having extra responsibility, for tax reasons. I sympathize with the suffragettes who had to see women not even bothering to vote. Plenty of other women could carry on with careers and babies, as I have done. Too many are feeble and unprepared to accept that it is possible to do two things at the same time properly.

To what extent are external factors to blame for the lack of women at the top?

In a male-dominated world there is now a growing acceptance that there are some capable women around, but the over forties at any rate find it difficult to accept that women in general have equal capabilities with men. It is the older generation that is still in charge. However, this will change when men get used to seeing around them women doing the same things as they are. But I may be forced to accept that many women do put other things first. We will see.

What can be done to improve the career position of women?

The Equal Rights Bill will allow equal entry to the professions : allowing women to do what they want. But will girls continue to hang back as they used to? If women will let it happen, it seems to me that true equality could come about in five or ten years.

What advice would you give to girls who want to have children and a satisfying career?

Don't pull out thinking you can get back when you want to. Insist on maternity leave.

What advantages have you found in combining a family and career and what disadvantages?

It is what I always wanted and it has been pretty well all gain. Perhaps I have been lucky in so far as my firm has always valued its employees, both men and women, and been flexible about working hours. For instance it is quite understood if men take time off for their children's sports days too.

You need an iron constitution but even so you get tired. I have missed out on a few small things, like being at home when the children came back from school. But I have never missed anything important. I think that I would have forfeited many family things including, perhaps, the having of a family at all, if I had stayed in journalism and had not been able in some degree to control my own times and conditions of work.

What changes would you like to see in the future?

I would like to see allowances for housekeepers and I cannot see why not. I have a worried feeling that women are still being taxed unfairly despite separate assessment which looked good at first. Maternity leave by right for at least four months and generous payments. There are still anomalies in the Inland Revenue Rules of Procedure. I led the fight to get widowers treated in the same way as widows in the event of their working wife's death. That battle was won but there are still some discriminatory aspects of pensions.

HUSBAND'S COMMENTS

Can you single out any special qualities possessed by your wife which have enabled her to successfully combine family life with a demanding career?

Independence. Determination. Strong constitution.

What effect, would you say, has your wife's professional involvement had on your life as a family?

More money for a more interesting and enjoyable life. Marriage more of a partnership.

In the light of your own experience at home (and possibly at work) do you think it is realistic to expect an increase in the number of women who will put themselves forward to fill positions of high responsibility in the future?

Yes – definitely.

Mary Tuck, a Principal in the Home Civil Service, apologized for not offering her office as a meeting place, explaining that it would have been too distracting. She is tall, slim, and has a casual elegance. With her broad smile and direct speech, she is a person whom one trusts automatically and completely. Mary Tuck is the author of How Do we Choose? *in the Methuen Essential Psychology Series.*

Can you say what is most important in your life?

I need to think about things and I need people, equally. All my responsibilities are absolute. If I had to make choices between work responsibilities and people responsibilities, I'd have to devise some way of meeting both. Men have to. It's quite possible. It is wrong to be irresponsible about work because you have a family. Colleagues are people too.

I have always been confident about doing what I want, which is what I enjoy. If you are really asking me, the answer to the question is God. I am an intellectual person but I am also a religious person and that is the informing thing about me. I think women could do much more than they sometimes think.

How do you manage at home?

My husband and the four children – who are eighteen, fifteen, fourteen and nine – share in family decisions in a democratic way. Until recently I worked part-time; but it turned into full-time hours and working from home involved a lot of extra organizational strain. But it was important to me to be available to the children and also to get involved in community affairs.

I used to employ *au pairs*: one stayed six years, and most are still our friends. But it is a relief not to have anyone living in and the extra bedroom is useful.

I could not go out to work having a nine-year-old if I didn't have older children. After school, the older ones keep an eye on the youngest, in turns. He is left on his own very occasionally but that doesn't worry me, perhaps because I was brought up among people who had to work and know children can be responsible quite young if they know the situation. They like being grown-up. We live in a terrace with very friendly neighbours which gives me a fall-back in emergencies, and we share a common garden. Having been involved in the community is an advantage now, though I sometimes feel badly that I haven't much time to help. I do think the loss to the community would be terrible if all women went out to work.

I have two cleaning ladies, one old and one young, who do different things in the house and come every morning. The children all let themselves in in the afternoon. I am usually home at six and then cook family dinner which we normally eat together about eight. If I am out they use take-away food or meals I have left in the deep-freeze, but that is broken down at the moment!

I like cooking and we entertain a lot. I methodically set about filling a new deep-freeze before starting this full-time job. Cooking is second nature to me after all these years, feeding people is not that complicated. I was nervous about coping with a full-time job to begin with and it would have been out of the question if it hadn't been within one half-hour of home by public transport and if the leave arrangements hadn't been generous and adaptable enough to allow for taking the odd day off for sports days and things. I took a day off last week to cook for a large dinner party. In fact the Civil Service allows me somewhat more generous leave than my husband, who is a business executive, gets. The really big test comes with summer holidays. My husband and I are going to take turns having the children for spells at our cottage. Later we will take a holiday on our own, leaving the eldest in charge. The older ones make independent arrangements now, and then there is scout camp and visits to granny, so I think it will work out very well. I have found that having the infrastructure that goes with a big office is an enormous boon. It is so much easier to go to an office and be organized. Although I was used to running my own business, the entrepreneurial aspects were not enjoyable because I am not fundamentally interested in making money.

What are the problems?

The problems arise from my temperament and not from the work situation. I get depressed if a member of the family is ill, or gloomy. I can't help having a certain tension. For instance, after each baby I tried staying home, but found that after about six months I got bored. I am miserable without some intellectual task and have no creative feelings about housework the way some women do – though I think I am quite a good cook. What I really like is writing and thinking. When I go on a fortnight's course shortly I know the family will manage slightly less well without me, but I cannot feel guilty about it. I confess to a slightly naughty pleasurable feeling at running away with a good excuse.

Can you say how you have achieved success in your career?

I would undoubtedly have been more successful if I had stuck to one job. But I have been frivolous in some ways and done what I liked – which is the tremendous advantage that middle-class married women have. Many men would long for the chance to change jobs every few years. Before I joined the Civil Service last year, through open examination, I worked as an independent consultant, after taking an M.Sc. in my mid-thirties.

My working life took off again when I went back to study. I have always liked being a student, particularly when I have had enough money. The consequence of this highly successful study was my gaining a whole new credibility as a competent person. I could have returned to an academic career and I have slight regrets about that, but I am restricted by lack of mobility – I cannot go where the jobs are.

Problem solving is what I really enjoy. At the moment I am working well within my capacity – which is I think typical of the Civil Service, regrettably. The whole outfit is overstaffed with the result that a lower level of responsibility prevails than at a comparable salary level in business. I think a whole tier, a whole echelon, could go, with benefit, but you must remember I am quite new to the Service, so I can't make final judgements.

I enjoy what I am doing at the moment; for instance, preparing answers to Parliamentary questions and enquiries from Members. This involves examining the history, the precedents, and surrounding legislation, the union background perhaps, and all this information has to be digested, sorted, and turned into an elegant memorandum.

It is important to realize that it is experience that is valued above all else when promotion is being considered. Retraining is all very well, but it is less valued than the typical unbroken pattern of experience of males. My male contemporaries are Under Secretaries. Until men have the freedom to move about that women have, I do not think this will change. You need an awful lot of luck but it also helps to be on the inside; there are a lot of jobs you can't latch on to unless you are on the spot to know about them. Women themselves may know that they can catch up quickly, but this is not generally realized and they are disadvantaged in not having the unbroken years of experience.

I have always had the self-confidence not to think it was odd if a wife worked. The Lancashire women in my family never expected to give up public life for the domestic. My mother's example has been extremely important – she was widowed and went out to work when my brother and I were young. The fact that I am not convention-bound has helped me and I do not look for problems. But I only work hard if I am interested enough.

My new full-time career in the Civil Service came about because I was attracted by an advertisement for direct entry to Principal status aged thirty to fifty-two: how often do you see that age range? I am presently earning around £7,000 and will apply in due course for further responsibilities. Apparently I was one of thirty taken on of four hundred who applied. I was attracted by a job in central London that offered good pay and security. It may be cynical, but it seems to me that more and more work is going to be done in the public area, so one might as well join in. I think we are overgoverned and I regret it, but I think it is inevitable.

Are there advantages in being a woman in the Civil Service?

No, equality prevails; arithmetic has no sex. But I do think women have special qualities to bring to any profession. It is not a question of their femininity so much as the conditions of a woman's life : she is in touch with the whole area of life and its ongoing processes, she is more emotionally extended through her family. This means that less of her emotion is invested in her work status, whereas a man's life is less defined by his private life and more by his public life, which makes him more vulnerable. That's why women tend to be nicer than men : their experience as mothers teaches them to be unselfish; having children is a moral education.

Are there disadvantages?

One is busier, of course, having children, but that is enjoyable and worth it. There is no sex prejudice in promotion in the Civil Service – in fact it might almost be working the other way. The Service has a conscious policy of helping women over leave and things like that. I do not think there should be discrimination in their favour.

Do women disadvantage themselves?

A lot of fault lies in ourselves. The middle-class wife is the last luxuried class and too few make the best of it : it should be seen as a pleasure and an opportunity rather than a groan.

Women can do much more than they think. I realize that much of this stems from upbringing : there is a lack of work tradition for women in the middle class and a lack of confidence from family assumptions of inequality.

To what extent are external factors to blame for the lack of women at the top?

Women often make excuses when they are really doing what they want. I know many women who have refused promotion, fearful of taking more responsibility. In fact, the more senior you are, the easier it is to adjust your work to suit yourself. But women lose promotion opportunities because they are not around at the right time, because they can't match the long years of experience on the job that a man has.

What can be done to improve the career position of women?

A greater willingness to accept that learning acquired early on is valid and less overvaluing of work experience. New skills can be acquired more quickly than is generally thought. The Equal Opportunities Bill will help working-class women by doubling their money, giving them a chance to be navvies instead of chambermaids, road sweepers instead of waitresses. The pay is better and I doubt if the physical strain is more. But it would be wrong to discriminate in favour of women; promotion must be impartial, otherwise we will get a backlash.

What advice would you give to girls who want to have children and a satisfying career?

It is very tempting for women not to bother when they can see for themselves at an early age that they can have a perfectly good short-term career just being admired and then being kept by a husband. But it has been observed truly that the best marriages are the ones that don't have to stay together. In my experience it is self-respecting women who make good marriages. I would urge them to get themselves educated, to get a trade, skill, anything. And I would say marry when you fall in love and determine you're going to do your best to make it a success, your commitment for life. There's no best time to marry. It's when you see the man you want and he wants you. Trying to control everything by some pre-arranged plan is no way to live. Life is unpredictable. I think being too organized is a bad way to live; I dislike overplanning.

Females possess this subconscious knowledge that they don't have to make any sort of public career, they can live entirely at home, and this curbs ambition. It's no good just being the second sex, girls should put their value in what they can do, not how they are seen. In the end no one else is going to justify your existence. You have to do the job yourself.

Can you sum up the advantages and disadvantages of combining a family and career in your life?

Family life is more constraining than work life; it can gain from having the tougher side of the female nature being exercised at work. In a work situation women are more free to express all aspects of themselves : they can argue and be aggressive if necessary. It is good for us not to have to show always the kind, giving side of our nature that we need to exercise at home. Women can get carried too far into habits of unselfishness and then feel martyred. I can be much nicer to my family when I've had a good fierce, technical, no-holds-barred argument at work. The extra income is important too, to help pay for university education with a fair size family and a father's income which puts grants out of court. Clever over-eighteens are expensive for middle-class families these days.

I don't think fatigue is a problem if you enjoy your life; it is more usual to get tired if you don't have enough interesting things to do.

What changes would you like to see in future?

We need to rethink radically educational policy and change career patterns at the same time. Education should not be the routine finishing school for the young it is now. It should be thought of as long-term, to be taken up easily when it is wanted. A voucher system might work well, with so much for free and the rest to be worked and saved for. People should be able to change direction when they want to, and this would help to break the thirty- to forty-year unbroken work pattern that most men are trapped in. Too many young people go into further education now at eighteen because they are scared of missing the opportunity for ever. If they could do their three-year study whenever they wanted to, at any age, it might be better. I'd like to see forty-year-old men or women able to go to university or polytechnic to train to do something else.

But whatever changes are made in the system, I think there will always be a difference in the working patterns of men and women : women after all bear the babies and are designed to give suck. We actually like these things – at least I did. I think someone should be at home full-time with the under-fives and mothers seem the obvious people to do it. They enjoy it more; they are physically and genetically adapted to it. It was my womb which contracted when my babies cried, not my husband's. Women's Lib tends to see it as a deprivation that women have to stay with their young. But lots of women like to do so and are good at it. The children need someone, why not them? I was grateful to have a husband who would keep me and the children when they were young. My mother was a mother I had to do without. I valued the chance to have myself and my babies kept by a loving father. Women get rewards for their domestic period later, in a closeness with their children through the years of having been with them. Men miss too much of that. It is hard on them. They are out of the house too continuously. The way to get men to share domestic life more is not to bully and nag them, but get them to realize how much they *miss* in family contact if they are absent too much.

I look forward to seeing more equality in the way the two sexes balance private and public life. It shouldn't be all public life for men, all private for women. I cannot foresee the economic upheaval this would entail and I am pessimistic about career equality between the sexes becoming widespread. I think biology means women will always have to give slightly more time to domestic life, taking a lifetime as a whole.

HUSBAND'S COMMENTS

Can you single out any special qualities possessed by your wife which have enabled her to successfully combine family life with a demanding career?

Recurrent boredom with the conventional 'rewards' of family life. Being a great deal over-educated. A determination to live in central London. Escapism. And, in all modesty, *me*.

What effect, would you say, has your wife's professional involvement had on your life as a family?

It has left the children feeling that a mother is a father is a mother. The division between work and play becomes hazy. It has produced a long generation of *au pairs*, lovely continental waifs who usually needed another mother and father. The family becomes increasingly Russian : 'Who is this mad lady wandering about the house?'

In the light of your own experience at home (and possibly at work) do you think it is realistic to expect an increase in the number of women who will put themselves forward to fill positions of high responsibility in the future?

Women will continue, exponentially, to take power when and if it suits them. This is a matter not of personal experience but of statistics, sociology, education, birth control, democracy, masochism, sense of humour. What's more, it won't be half as overt as 'putting themselves forward to fill positions of high responsibility'. That is what they did in Victorian and Edwardian novels. Now they have to compete, lie, even work, like the rest of us. And, probably rightly, they will mainly ignore the House of Commons.

Dorothy Tutin is an unstagy person, relaxed and friendly. Only her resonant, slightly husky voice, and her vivacious face, might lead one to guess that she is a celebrated actress. Her half turned-out cupboard was abandoned as we settled to talk in the sunshine of her pretty garden, while the black dog stretched out on the grass and her daughter Amanda, ill with glandular fever, watched us from her bed in the adjacent playroom.

Can you say what is most important in your life?

Family naturally. I even thought I could give up acting when I was having the children. Nature took over: it was exciting and absorbing; there was no question of problems or decisions or sacrifices. I was thrilled with having them and with feeding them. It's good to feel so useful.

I am reminded of the time I got the doctor's permission to leave my breast-fed first-born for thirty-six hours so that I could join the tercentenary Shakespeare celebrations going on in Rome; I suspect I'm the only person to have expressed milk in the Vatican! When I got back I found my baby had refused a bottle throughout my absence. As I rushed home from the airport nobody even asked me about the Pope.

I did have my children late. I think it is different for younger actresses who often want to get back to the theatre as fast as they can. But for me, having had children gave me a sense of fulfilment. In fact, as I said, for a time I didn't think I wanted to act. But as they grew up, after nine months or so, I discovered that I did need to act after all. I was taken by surprise; it seemed acting was a necessity for me – a therapy perhaps.

How do you manage at home?

I thought that if I was going to enjoy my children I must have someone to help me, and so we did employ a girl even when I wasn't working. We've had a lot of *au pairs*, fascinating ones sometimes, but when the last one just didn't come back we were thankful; it is so nice to have the house to ourselves and I do think we can manage now that they are nine and eleven. I do know I shouldn't have liked a trained nanny; we tried one once in an emergency, but you can't have other people telling you how to deal with your own children. I went to the children's clinic if I needed advice.

My husband being an actor is a great help and luckily we usually keep different hours. But I have always avoided being away more than one week at a time. I do assume the main responsibility for the household and do not, I think, expect as much of him when he is working hard as I do of myself. But I am learning to ease up a bit; for instance he likes to cook and is actually better at it than I am so I am getting used to not feeling guilty about that. There is teatime. Children coming home feel all bounce and vitality, and if you are working in the theatre it is from teatime onwards that you need most energy, so there is a problem of conserving it for the performance. So – much as I would like to be freer then, I am already beginning to separate myself. I think the children understand and excuse my 'abstraction'. I have often taken them to the theatre, so there can be no mystery about what I do when I am away from them.

We have never sent the children away. On our big trip to America when Derek and I were acting together, we took the children with us. We also took an Australian help who fell in love two days before we left and went to pieces. I shall never forget the journey to Los Angeles through Kennedy Airport, looking for the crèche (just a slab as it turned out), and nobody coping but me. But I would not have gone without them. Of course I couldn't take on an engagement like that now because I wouldn't dream of disturbing their schooling. In any case I avoid long engagements away. I would miss them.

What are the problems?

When the show *has* to go on. The worst was when my daughter had measles very badly and I had to play a matinee of *Peter Pan* – of all things. I rang up at every interval. Luckily my husband could be there. *Having* to go to work – no matter what – is certainly a problem for a mother. Then there's the routine of domestic chores – that gets tedious. I am happy to do anything once and don't mind doing things in one fell swoop – and I enjoy having a clear-out between jobs as I am doing today – but I have a low tolerance of domestic chores. I am learning now not to rush, and therefore I do things better.

Finding the uninterrupted time to concentrate. I had not realized before I had children how much of the day I spent thinking about a role. One's train of thought is unavoidably interrupted, and I do find it difficult. But there is a bonus; my children are now old enough to hear my lines, which they do marvellously well and I find it invaluable. So what you lose on the swings . . .! In many respects television, which is generally a nine-to-five job, has fewer problems and if, as I experienced recently, you do a series where you record for three days once a fortnight away from home, that surprisingly makes life much easier. It is simply a matter of preparing food, etc., before you go and, once away, it is just you and the play and coping with the technical problems involved. I find working in the theatre more difficult. Rehearsals are more arduous and the problems more profound.

Can you say how you have achieved success in your career?

I have been extraordinarily lucky. I didn't want to be an actress to begin with and I never did charades at home or anything like that – except a bit at school which I left early after giving up the idea of a career in music. But my father and mother both loved the theatre and thought it would be good for me, since I was shy and self-conscious. However it soon dawned on me what an incredibly difficult art it was, with only one's self as the instrument. I nearly gave up because although I lacked confidence I also desperately wanted to be good at whatever I did. My mother, however, insisted that if I had high standards for myself that was an advantage and to be coped with, and she persuaded me to carry on. I was never a startling pupil. I generally played maids and little boys. I was sent from RADA to audition for a small part in a club theatre and I was, amazingly, offered the leading part. After that, like any actress, my career came and went; a year at Bristol Old Vic playing juveniles, followed by a year of walk-on parts and understudying at the Old Vic in London. Then there was a dismal period, followed by real good fortune – three parts in a row in the West End. So many actresses do not have the opportunity to act leading roles while they are still young, and they lose confidence. Our profession is overcrowded. I know I have been lucky; but then anyone can be lucky with the will to concentrate and to regard *everything* one performs, however insignificant, as important. I have also learned through my children. The haughtiness of my daughter as a baby was a great help for Queen Victoria, and though I hope I should have had the imagination to feel my way into Peter Pan, having a six-year-old boy on hand, living only for the moment, did help.

Are there any advantages in being a woman in your profession?

There is no difference. It happens that the fashion of the moment is for plays with lots of men's parts. Maybe if more women were writing there would be more parts for women, but that is a large subject. If anything, I would say that acting is a harder career for a man. A woman after all does not have to feel the same striving after greatness that men commonly have, and she may not have the same desire to achieve a high position. It is more socially acceptable for a woman to be at the struggling stage. God knows it is a hard profession whether one fails or succeeds, but we have all chosen it knowing the hazards.

Are there disadvantages?

It is terribly difficult to combine family life with acting if you are not in a position to refuse parts in out of the way places. You may be able to travel with your family when they are little but not when they are in school. There is a lot to be said for putting off having children until you are well established in your profession, and I think you may even value them more highly because they are then an added joy to your life and not taking something away.

Do you think that women disadvantage themselves?

I do not quite know what you mean. If you mean that we do not fulfil our potential I quite agree with you. But in a rush for this so-called equality I think we are in danger of out-pacing ourselves and antagonizing and frightening men. Women need men in the widest possible sense! Of course women should have the same opportunities but we are so totally different and we should seek the best and kindest way. I think women are even more unattractive than men when they are aggressive and bossy; I think it is against their nature, one can laugh at a man. We have had an idiotic system that has held women back and kept them at home, but we must move more slowly, be patient. Of course we must find a better place in the sun and most men want to help. But we can do this without losing our inherent compassion and understanding. In my experience the 'best men' naturally think women are 'equal'. I am aware that there is an underground that hasn't changed, but I am afraid of extremes.

To what extent are external circumstances to blame for the lack of women at the top?

I think that women *want* to look up to men and *can* feel fulfilled in helping a man to be inventive and creative at the sacrifice of developing some of their abilities. But it is curious that many women were prominent in Victorian times and in the Suffragette Movement, and yet there was no follow-through. In the generation before us many women had leisure and domestic help (even those not particularly well-off), yet careers for married women were frowned on. The women who did work were poor, and perhaps the difference between forced labour and dilettante occupations prevented positive progress in the area of hard-working, long-studying dedication to a career. I wonder if part of the explanation is that women don't want men to feel threatened.

What can be done to improve the career position of women?

Education. The sense of total equality must come from teachers. Girls need a particular encouragement if they are to achieve. They forge ahead in the earlier years and I think they are more malleable than boys. But at the stage when they could be planning a career many girls flag. I think this is a *natural* phenomenon and that teachers should tell them so. Maybe they should be allowed to take time off to work on some project, anything to keep the mind working, and then have the opportunity to come back and try for academic attainment if they want to. Boys don't need this cooling-off stage so much – they start slower and then forge ahead. Some way must be found to increase the potential of everyone. I'm sure we should find new ways of testing and not make it so difficult for people who failed or missed their opportunities (so often women) to try again.

I also think that the professions in which women shine, like nursing and teaching, have outmoded hierarchies; they must be altered to fit the life-style of working mothers, and they must encourage women to take more responsibility. Crèches should be provided for study as well as for jobs, but I am not at all in favour of child dumping.

What advice would you give to girls who want to have children and a satisfying career?

I should hate my own daughter not to have both career and family, but how to manage both is a serious problem which must be thought out. I would say: put off having children until you are established, if possible, and then they will add to your life without depriving you. It is essential to take time off to maintain close contact for at least nine months. If you lose contact there is physical loss on both sides. It is such a short time and if you are frightened of being trapped at home, think positively that this is a blessed time that men *can't* have, a time when you can think, write, read, sew, or learn to play the flute! It is no use thinking a woman can lead a life like a man; to bear a child is not like laying an egg to be brooded over later by someone else. Close contact must go on as they grow up, but not all day everyday.

Can you sum up the advantages and disadvantages of combining family and career in your life?

My father used to say, 'When two people ride a donkey, one must ride behind.' Sharing is always a problem but it does help if one can look at it humorously. If anything is amiss at home I automatically feel guilty and I think women have an inborn guilt where children are concerned.

In some ways my career and children are quite separate – I'm not one of those who wants pictures of the children around in my dressing room – but family life does give one a better sense of proportion. Having them with us when we were travelling stopped us fussing and took the edge off our fears. It doesn't alter my last-minute nerves, but they do give me a perspective about everything else, and any professional decision I make has to be related to the whole family.

What changes would you like to see in future?

Radical changes in education are crucial as I have said. Women need special encouragement because it is very hard for a woman to push herself. But I think it is worthwhile because many men would enjoy a more equal existence – it would be less burden on them for instance.

*Phyllis Willmott received me in her pleasant office in a Queen
Anne house overlooking Victoria Square, Bethnal Green, where
she works in a social research institute four days a week. She is
neat, youthful and charming, without self-consciousness, and has
a warm and unassuming manner. Mrs Willmott is consultant to
the Family Day Centre Projects financed by the EEC under their
anti-poverty programme. Her researches into the social services
at the Institute of Community Studies have always focused on
the consumer; her* Consumers' Guide to the Social Services *has
become the reference work in the field. She is also on a working
party of the Personal Social Services Council and writes for* New
Society.

Can you say what is most important in your life?

I think family: I have an incredibly happy marriage and I
adore my two sons. Personal fulfilment through work is also
important.

How do you manage at home?

The boys who are now grown-up are still at home quite often,
I'm glad to say: sometimes I think we moved into a small house
too soon. I took a career break for five years, starting with the
birth of my first. I had thought I would go back to work straight
away and get a neighbour in or something but in fact I felt I
would not find care of a good enough standard and I was put
off by Bowlby. I admit I didn't like being at home entirely and
found it lonely and frustrating but by the time my second child
was born I was more accepting. My husband has been a fantastic
help: he has always been a feminist and practises what he
preaches. He undertook to do night duty with the second baby

after I had had a hard time with the first who was wakeful and active all the time : it got to the point where both children would call out for daddy in the night. My husband really came to believe in sharing the care of the children after beginning as a matter of practical necessity. I employed cleaning help only (a man who was excellent, one day a week): this was a matter of economics but also I have always felt somehow disapproving about *au pairs* and most helps because they come and go. My husband has never needed much looking after : I don't think in our domestic roles we have a rigid sex differentiation but we do tend to think of the car and the care of it as his responsibility and cooking as mine. He likes to shop and will go to the launderette. He pays the bills although we have a joint account of course. I think I force him into taking the major domestic decisions because I am lazy and do not think so much ahead. Basically the chores are shared according to temperament.

What are the problems?

When the children were at home, especially up to seven before they had outgrown that endless ailment stage, going out to work even part-time was a struggle because I felt I had to constantly prove my reliability as a workmate. Getting them to school was sometimes a terrible trial because one child had almost a school phobia phase, very difficult to deal with. Later, in their teens, I chose to work at home and took four years over one important project : a long time but they frequently needed me then too. For a long time I staggered from school holiday to school holiday and I often thought how nice it would be if more women could share my fortune of finding jobs that stop for the holidays.

Can you say how you have achieved success in your career?

I was ambitious from the start – although I think I am much less so now. My family influence was important, I was a girl among four boys. I felt that my mother's treating me differently, like expecting me to always set the table, was unfair. I had to prove I was as good as the boys.

I was an early leaver from grammar school, where I was unhappy and self-conscious about my working-class background.

Besides, I didn't want to be a teacher, carrying on in the environment I disliked, which was the only profession my parents could visualize for me. I was very good at some things like botany and art and dim at others like French. I went to work at the Times Book Club. After the war I applied for medical social work training, partly because I didn't have the nerve to ask to do medicine. Later it was my husband's encouragement that pushed me on : he was always in favour of one's being oneself. I was diligent but not particularly energetic. I had to drive myself originally. Nowadays I have less interest or will for being at the front and have turned down jobs which would be too demanding. I enjoy having a little influence in my field but I want also to keep my freedom to enjoy other interests, which is perhaps selfish.

Are there advantages to being a woman in your profession?

Social work has always been regarded as a woman's profession but this is changing as it is becoming relatively well paid and with an improved career structure. Women have found openings in social work because it has been underpaid and undervalued but I am glad to say this is changing rapidly. I think women may have kidded themselves that only they have the special skills for social work but from my contacts with male social work students I am convinced they can be just as 'caring' and interested in the deeply personal way regarded as a feminine attribute. Women will continue to enter in large numbers but it does not look as if they will stay – two or three years is the average at the moment. All the signs are that men will enter in increasing numbers and they will stay in and go up to the top. Look how many men are Directors of Social Services (the top of the profession) already. I think we can expect to see more men enter nursing for the same reasons although in that case doctoring will continue to attract the more talented of both sexes.

Are there disadvantages?

It is difficult to combine social work with family especially at top levels, and when the children are young. The opposing pressures are too great. We will not see many women Directors of Social Service.

Do women disadvantage themselves?

Of course – by getting married and having families. Many women don't make the top because of the break in their careers.

To what extent are external factors to blame for the lack of women at the top?

The dice are still loaded against them. For instance, selection procedures are based on the notion that women will give up and so they are kept out. This means, unfortunately, that even those women who do want an unbroken career and who are ambitious, are penalized. And this partly because of the women who are happier to settle for 'a bit of both worlds'.

What can be done to improve the career position for women?

Women have to give up work at the young-children stage normally because it is so difficult to do both. The necessity for a career break should be accepted although I think the price women pay is that they will not get the top jobs; but for many this is an advantage rather than otherwise. More day care facilities is not really an answer because in their hearts most women feel that communal care is not ideal for little children. I do think there should be more willingness to care for children where their mothers work but it cannot be done without proper arrangements and needs organizing. Better trained home helps are no answer if they are unlikely to stay: the trouble is they get married and leave too. Older women might be an answer. Men could help more if their hours were more flexible: more men would enjoy sharing the care of their children if they had the opportunity.

What advice would you give to girls who want to have children and a satisfying career?

It is easy to say put off having children, although getting quali-

fications and experience before the break is important. I feel
sorry for the young now who have a real choice to make about
whether to have children and when. I had both my children
almost by accident : we assumed we would and there is no deny-
ing the urge to reproduce yourself is there if you have a con-
genial mate. I think we were lucky to have had the pleasurable
alternative of being allowed to be 'carried away'. This is no
longer so easy as the chanciness has been removed from contra-
ception by the Pill. You lose an awful lot, a whole dimension, if
you do not have children. But you must be your own person. If
you take a career break to look after them – and you give up a
lot if you give up the early mothering role – you should keep
your hand in. The period when you are looking in two directions
can be long – teenage children need your time and energy too.
But you may be able to put on a spurt later or you may feel you
have a better life for not aiming at the top job. We are inclined
to forget that men do pay a price for the demanding 'top job' –
and sometimes this is at the cost of the deeper rewards the
parental role can offer.

What changes would you like to see in the future?

Leaving aside the need for more and *better* day care, I think,
firstly more flexible career patterns for men and women : that is,
more opportunity to break off and to change direction for both
sexes. Secondly more sharing of the family care. It is these two
things which will, if at all, break the vicious cycle. If men, as
well as women, take 'career breaks' this would no longer be seen
as a reason for 'blocking' top jobs just to women. Or alternatively
it would no longer be seen as the inevitable and desirable end for
the man to be the ambitious one and the woman not to be.
Similarly, the more men are involved in family care the more
they will benefit – and this doesn't mean turning 'Daddy' into
just another kind of 'Mummy'.

So to sum up, I do feel strongly that we should be aiming towards enabling people of either sex to develop their own personally suitable pattern of family life. It is not really whether a
woman has a career break or not, or a top job or not, which is
important. It's getting the choice right and understanding what

the advantages and the disadvantages of any choice mean, and not just for any particular period in life – say when the children are small – but over the whole span.

HUSBAND'S COMMENTS

Can you single out any special qualities possessed by your wife which have enabled her to successfully combine family life with a demanding career?

Her ability plus some ambition.

What effect, would you say, has your wife's professional involvement had on your life as a family?

It has involved some stress, obviously, but then so has any 'professional involvement'. On balance, it has worked out well.

In the light of your own experience at home (and possibly at work) do you think it is realistic to expect an increase in the number of women who will put themselves forward to fill positions of high responsibility in the future?

Personal observation and my work as a sociologist point to 'yes'. It is an historical trend, reinforced by – and expressing – a change in the family and sexual roles.

Dr X Y, who asked to remain anonymous for professional reasons, is a vivacious person with a striking smile. Although she practises at home, there is no trace of the consulting room in her spacious and comfortable living quarters. So busy that she could offer only a patient's cancelled appointment for an interview, she nevertheless was able to relax and reflect.

What is most important in your life?

My family. My work and my training have always been geared around my family.

How did you manage a home and a career?

My husband has always been a great help. He spent a lot of time with the boys when they were young. He used to supervise their homework and read them stories at bedtime when I was training. I also had a close friend with boys of the same age. We used to exchange children twice a week on alternate days. One always walked a tight-rope of guilt – worried that the cricket shorts were not white enough! I, like so many working mothers, tended to over-compensate. I never missed a sports day or any other school occasion. Of course some things had to go. I was never able to meet friends for coffee or lunch, or to wander around exhibitions. Now that I could do this, I don't know how to any more. Perhaps loneliness goes side by side with success when the children move away.

How has this affected your career?

In medicine one can fortunately move around. I opted out of full-time hospital jobs when I got married, and when my sons were born I began to practise privately by appointment at home. I lost a range of possibilities, but couldn't have done the full-time hospital work necessary for the next stage. It would have been emotionally impossible for me. I did however keep two clinical assistant posts in dermatology at two hospitals throughout this time and until I became a qualified psychoanalyst.

How have you achieved success in your career?

I came from a family in which it was expected that we all do something academic. My mother was a doctor and all my aunts, both maternal and paternal, went to university. Even my teenage revolt took the form of reading modern languages first instead of medicine. Later I began to cook, after I was married, and I looked after my children myself. In my mother's circle academic women didn't do domestic things or take any interest in clothes, and they had nannies for their children.

Although it was expected that I have a profession like my brothers, I was not expected to reach the top. I think my parents would have been astonished to see what I am doing today. It was my mother, mainly, who kept me at work after my first child was born. She not only encouraged me, but actually came and stayed with the baby for the hours I worked at hospital – two half-days a week. I would have been happy to stay at home at that point. It is interesting that I have always needed to be pushed into things by others, first by my mother and then by my colleagues who have thrust things upon me. I am not a volunteer. My father too very much encouraged me to keep up my professional life, since my mother had not and he thought it was a pity.

How have you found motherhood combines with a career?

I think everything depends on the age of the children and the amount of one's investment in them. In the early years, the only creative thing I did was to take care of my home and children. It was not until the boys left home that I was able to find another channel for my creativity. And then I was asked. That was how I discovered that I had something to say and that there were people eager to listen to me. I think a mother can only expand at the same rate as her children, and that rate varies even between children in the same family. If one thrusts a false independence on children too early, for one's own wishes, they are less likely to be able to cope with difficulties in later years. On the other hand if one does not develop areas in one's own life, it becomes hard for a mother to let her children separate when they are ready. If her investment in the children is too great, she will tend to suffocate them and to suffer from menopausal depressions herself. Motherhood is a growing and diminishing process. It seems to me that it is important to be available but not demanding – a difficult task!

In the light of your experience what changes would you like to see in the future in the pattern of life at work and in the home?

In my experience self-employment was a major advantage in my own life, since I could adjust my working life around my family duties and pleasures. My husband was extremely helpful and it seems to me that equally for these husbands who enjoy sharing family duties self-employment is very useful. I also think that shortage of domestic help and indeed the anxiety that most mothers feel in trusting their children to strangers should be considered by employers who wish to retain the advantages of women working. For instance flexible working hours and play groups or crèches which would care for children at their mothers' employment would be a help in keeping women at work at least part time while their children are young, gradually increasing the hours as the children grow.

I would also like to see young women intent on a professional life trained to do domestic chores efficiently and well from their schooldays as I certainly was not, and encouraged to finish their training before their children are born. I would like to see provision made in my own profession for many opportunities for part-time work even when the children are young, since it seems to me that without keeping abreast of modern developments in even a limited sphere middle-aged women returning to work will always be at a disadvantage.

HUSBAND'S COMMENTS

Can you single out any special qualities possessed by your wife which have enabled her to successfully combine family life with a demanding career?

Innumerable qualities but perhaps the most important are ambition and the talents necessary to fulfil it, balance, and an ability to listen.

What effect, would you say, has your wife's professional involvement had on your life as a family?

Negatively, very little, as she always worked at home and so kept good contact with the children. Positively, by preventing over-care and over-devotion; and by making her stimulating and an object of pride. It has also improved the living standard.

In the light of your own experience at home (and possibly at work), do you think it is realistic to expect an increase in the number of women who will put themselves forward to fill positions of high responsibility in the future?

Women should be encouraged to take more responsible jobs, especially where her 'husband' is willing to do a full share of the household work, or where she has no family.

III

III

The Need for Change

At a time of rapid change, when every kind of habit and custom is being reappraised, the pattern of women's employment is also shifting. The proportion of women who marry and work is rising and public rejection of the old-style role of the housewife is all but universal.

At the same time, the acquisition of training and expertise is becoming more costly. It is therefore of the utmost importance to society to avoid the wastage of skilled and experienced personnel, especially as people of top calibre in the work force are always in short supply. Yet this waste is evident in the case of countless married women who find themselves unable to contribute their talents to the labour market because of family commitments.

The Equal Pay and Equal Opportunities legislation will hasten change and improve status and prospects for women at all levels. But at the core of the movement towards greater opportunities is women's commitment to family care.

The claims of a career and those of a family need not be mutually exclusive : the evidence contributed to this book suggests that, on the contrary, one enhances and reinforces the other. But certain restrictions have to be accepted as natural and inevitable, such as a woman's tendency to give precedence to her husband's career needs. For example, women at a distance from urban centres find their career choices narrowed regardless of their husbands' financial support, which can include something as fundamental as the provision of transport.

Nevertheless, a number of other factors which at present restrict women's work opportunities, especially those precluding the upward movement to work of higher responsibility, could be eliminated. The purpose, here, of examining ways and means of enabling women to work with a greater degree of freedom is to differentiate between those restrictions that are necessary and those that could usefully be done away with.

In 1977 the restrictions are so comprehensive that women who 'go out' to work tend to be concentrated in areas of employment where the lowest rates of pay prevail, and in jobs that carry the lowest status and responsibility.

Increasing self-consciousness among women everywhere is already creating demand for more educational resources; but fields of employment accessible to women are still restricted and generally confined to service-oriented occupations and non-managerial work in commerce and industry.

If higher productivity is the key to economic progress, every encouragement to the female half of the population to enter higher brackets of employment – and of taxpaying – would seem self-evidently desirable. But this objective must be reconciled with a woman's family and community function, which is of prime importance to most women.

The 'dropping out' of the mother with a young family seems to be here to stay. But it need not always be equated with permanent retirement, and when it is temporary, it should be regarded as a desirable contribution to the well-being of the whole community rather than a liability or a nuisance. Thus, ways and means to enable and encourage women to make a second start deserve to be given top priority in the social planning of the nation.

Fluidity of employment is beginning to be seen as a desirable objective for men. This should help to change the climate of opinion in favour of women moving more freely in and out of employment and joining training schemes at any time of their working lives. Work sharing and pairing, and concentration of working hours at certain times of the year to accommodate family need, should also become more common.

The prominence of single women – a legacy of two world wars – in top jobs has obscured the inevitability of recruiting married women, or men, to succeed them. Single-minded high flyers among women will always be conspicuous; they will become a rarity in what have been regarded as the feminine professions if, as is already happening, a higher proportion of women are also mothers.

The advantage of recruiting married women will become more

apparent as the number of single women in top jobs declines; their replacement by men is already common because of the shortage of qualified women applicants. In contradiction to the intention of current legislation the proportion of women in top jobs seems to be actually dwindling. The diminution of some of the practical obstacles that inhibit women from seeking responsibility outside the home should slow this trend and hasten the movement towards a more equable distribution of work at the top.

SOME PROPOSALS

We have seen earlier that, for a woman, the requirements of family life – that is, the carrying out of tasks normally expected of wives and mothers – often prove to be incompatible with advancement within the usual career structures. A few exceptional – or exceptionally lucky – women manage to get round the problems and to reach the top. But many never expect to achieve the targets for which their energy and talents would undoubtedly qualify them if they were free to pursue their careers in the same way that most men are.

We have claimed that the focus on the family situation is unlikely to change radically in the foreseeable future. But in the meantime there are a number of ways in which the gap between the twin targets of being a good wife and mother and succeeding in a career – still generally considered irreconcilable – can be narrowed.

Flexible hours, time away and part-time work

A few women manage to work unremittingly through the period when they would have preferred to spend more time with their children, or have the good fortune of having adaptable employers or being in professions where regular hours are not the norm. But these tend to be exceptional cases. As a general rule employers need to be encouraged to grant leave of absence more freely, and to introduce arrangements such as pairing and sharing of jobs as well as three- or four-day weeks. The initial difficulties are far outweighed by the long-term gains, as the growing number of organizations who are trying it can testify. Expansion has been slow, partly because of economic conditions which have discouraged experimentation, and partly because no concessions have been granted by Government, trade unions or professional bodies with respect to insurance, pensions and other benefits. Sticking to the rule book has kept many a good woman out.

Part-time, or less than full-time work, still has a bad name and yet it is the only solution to the compromise many women seek. There is likely to be a period in the lives of most women when working normal hours in a job puts an undesirable strain on the family. For many of those who are able to exercise choice, 'less than full-time' is a permanent solution. For some it is a transition to full-time but always full-time with flexibility.

Government, being itself the largest employer of women, must take the lead. Flexibility is being introduced increasingly in the Civil Service at national level, but far less at local level where work for women should be most accessible.

The Ministry of Employment actively discourages part-time work by failing to keep registers of any work that is not full-time (except for shift work), nor do its career advisory officers take part-time work seriously. Until the Ministry itself sets an example by encouraging part-time work, we cannot expect private institutions to do much more than experiment half-heartedly. A thorough investigation of this complex subject, with its immense scope for variation, is overdue.

The requirement of flexibility presents the greatest problem in management where continuity and availability on the job can be crucial. But this survey has underlined a fundamental point which is too often disregarded : flexible hours need not mean fewer hours. Women who want responsibility display endurance and a willingness to forgo leisure that few men would countenance. All the women in this survey who work this way have said that it is worthwhile. We must assume that there could be many more of them.

Lack of promotion

Women of ambition and talent, like other women, tend to with-draw at the age when men are beginning to forge ahead in their careers. If they want to have children, as most do, there is no obvious way round this dilemma. Careers, particularly in manage-ment but in many professional fields as well, are often blighted because talent for leadership must be actively demonstrated at an early stage, the very stage at which women are often absent having children. During this time, men are gaining expertise and experience in the job for which there is no substitute when promotion is being considered. Some women at the top say they never gave up, but that is neither possible nor desirable for everyone.

The remedy must be a radical one : to re-schedule training pro-grammes deliberately for so-called 'older' women (with increased life expectancy, employers should recognize that women might have as much as twenty years of working life ahead of them, even after their children are grown-up). For those women who prefer working part-time, there should be a deliberate concentration of training – and work-conferences – on certain days of the week and in the middle hours of the day. Women are excluded from many situations where decisions have to be made by simply not being there at the time. It is the unscheduled meeting, the over-seas conference, the extra appearance after hours, from which the married woman tends to be absent because she cannot man-age such extras without sacrificing her family life.

Child care

We have seen that career women prefer to take principal re-sponsibility for the care of their children. Very few of the women in this survey have completely delegated this to others, and the few who did – of necessity, at the baby stage – tend to regret it. It is therefore fair to assume that many women are deterred from embarking on a career in the first place because they do not find this particular solution satisfactory.

Other ways of solving the problem are, however, beginning to emerge : the provision of crèches and nursery schools sponsored by employers is inducing a number of women to return to work, and setting an example that can be followed. The playgroup movement, set up by women to help each other, has enabled many women to expand their horizons. But bringing up children does not end with the nursery years. It is a much more lengthy and demanding process than is generally recognized, and one that involves conscientious mothers into adolescence and beyond. The needs of the adolescent are different from those of the young child, but the mother still has a crucial part to play and, in some ways, is harder to replace. A three-year-old may make do with another familiar lap, but a worried sixteen-year-old requires adult concern and guidance which, often, the parents alone are qualified and available to give. One way of providing support during this extended stage is the provision of more weekly boarding schools – offering security and supervision without usurping the parental role – at lower cost than full-time boarding. Holiday camps, which have the added advantage that older children in the family can take some responsibility for the younger ones, are a useful solution for the long school holidays – often a nightmare for mothers whose work does not stop at the end of their children's term. Government registration and even sponsorship of day and boarding camps would work to everyone's benefit, relieving parents of the need for makeshift arrangements. They would also have the added advantage of helping children to acquire skills and self-reliance, and offer them the invaluable experience of forming relationships with other adults, ideally both men and women.

Other dependants

A woman's new-found ability to determine the size of her family will not help her to reduce other kinds of dependent relationships, such as the care of invalids and the aged. On the contrary, as the lives of the elderly lengthen, women's traditional feminine role of comforter of the old and infirm is likely to take over from the strictly maternal role, so that, in a sense, the chances are that she will never be entirely 'free'. Even if she finds ways of replacing her own frequent presence, the cost may be disproportionate. Community care, too, will put even more reliance on women in the home, and even more pressure on women in careers – although it is to be welcomed as an advance on total institutional care. As in the case of children, the answer lies in supplementing, rather than taking over, a woman's responsibilities. There will have to be more and better paid domiciliary day care to improve the general lowly image of the home help (a role in which some women see themselves unwillingly cast), and more resources will have to be devoted to geriatric needs, regardless of income. Hospital 'holidays' could become more prevalent, and weekly boarding could be tried for the infirm as well as the hale. In this way some of the pressure points and moments of intolerable strain, which are now unquestioningly accepted and borne by most women, could and should be mitigated.

The changing role of men

It is a fact that fathers are doing more mothering than they used to. The importance of their role in bringing up children is becoming more widely understood, and the rewards and pleasures are being discovered. However, on the evidence of this survey, the sharing of family responsibilities does not yet encompass acceptance of a reversal of roles. The career of the husband has invariably been given priority over that of the wife, because he is traditionally regarded as the principal provider, and there are times when someone has to be given precedence. Perhaps one will have to look to the next generation for a change in attitudes.

Lack of information and advice

Many of the issues that affect a woman's chance to work in the course of her life are often no more than a hazy notion to a young girl, faced with a number of career choices.

A change of interests or late realization of potential, which long-term leave of absence cannot cater for; overcrowding in certain professions and too rigid a career structure in others; the need to be where one's husband is – these are commonplace considerations on which women receive little information or guidance. A number of women in this survey stress the role that luck or chance have played in their professional lives, and – even allowing for modesty – the facts bear them out.

The remedy could lie in skilled and realistic careers advice for girls while still at school and at every later stage. The advantages, in terms of employment prospects, of training for a shortage profession or of acquiring specialist skills could be pointed out, for example. Similarly, a warning could be issued about those shortage professions that have become so because women have boycotted them (the paramedical professions are a classic example of understaffing because women have not been offered acceptable working hours or high enough pay).

National registration and training of careers advisers would be a welcome step, but here skill must go hand in hand with sympathy. Girls' schools are notoriously inept at careers advice, lacking built-in facilities for liaison with the outside world. The advertising and compulsory notification of all vacancies, including part-time ones, would also help to fill the information gap. Too much career information lies concealed and inaccessible, and opportunities are lost as a result. Even when they are not actively looking for employment, women need to be able to find out what is going on in order to prepare themselves.

Prejudice

Prejudice resulting in some form of discrimination seems to be one of the most ineradicable problems. Overt instances, such as the policy of a well-known merchandising company of not appointing women to the board of one of its department stores, will, one hopes, be tackled by the Equal Opportunities Commission. But usually instances are harder to pin down; even when the absence of women at the top of preponderantly female organizations becomes all too evident, for example, one cannot challenge the claim that promotion and 'approval' must be merited; certainly it cannot be bestowed by legislation.

In organizations where women are already established, openness and frankness in decision-taking processes must be encouraged. Women are frequently handicapped because consultations and meetings involving policy decisions take place when women are not around, as has been said earlier. Again, this cannot be remedied by legislation.

In industry and management, and in certain professions (e.g. some of the 'numerate' ones mentioned earlier) where equal opportunity for training and experience are vital but sometimes so hard to obtain that all but the most determined women are of necessity excluded, special help in the form of positive discrimination in their favour may be necessary. It is therefore important that the Equal Opportunities Commission allows the few existing schemes of this kind to continue.* Some industrial companies are already taking encouraging steps in this direction; both the British Steel Corporation and the British Oxygen Company, for example, have been active in this respect, attempting to promote women within their ranks as well as recruiting them from outside.†

Given goodwill, the restructuring of career patterns, the encouragement of the Equal Opportunities Commission and the practical solution of a number of problems already discussed, the drop-out rate of women should fall considerably and many more should succeed. The cycle of non-expectation will be broken once women are visible in numbers and are seen to be performing in positions of leadership because they are competent people, not exceptions to the rule.

---

* Several special schemes are run by the Industrial Society.

† In June 1974 the British Oxygen Company gathered twenty-five women executives together to discuss career opportunities and obstacles to their promotion in the company, and produced a programme of action for senior management. This workshop was regarded as a way of making the most effective use of national resources – an obvious approach but a rare one in practice. It was discovered that one of the important obstacles to promotion was a lack of experience in industrial relations negotiations, considered essential for general or non-specialist management; industry is failing to provide women with this experience, as are the trade unions. The workshop concluded that more shop-floor experience should be offered to women, and it also accepted that hidden female talent should be searched out in the ranks because women are often under-educated and undervalued.